GOOD WRITING FOR BUSINESS

CHANDOS BUSINESS GUIDES
BUSINESS SKILLS

Chandos Business Guides are designed to provide managers with practical, down-to-earth information. The Chandos Business Guides are written by leading authors in their respective fields. If you would like to receive a full listing of current and forthcoming titles, please visit our web site www.chandospublishing.com or contact Melinda Taylor on email mtaylor@chandospublishing.com or direct telephone number +44 (0) 1865 882727.

New authors: we are always pleased to receive ideas for new titles; if you would like to write a Chandos Business Guide, please contact Dr Glyn Jones on email gjones@chandospublishing.com or direct telephone number +44 (0) 1865 884447.

Bulk orders: some organisations buy a number of copies of our books. If you are interested in doing this, we would be pleased to discuss a discount. Please contact Dr Glyn Jones on email gjones@chandospublishing.com or direct telephone number +44 (0) 1865 884447.

GOOD WRITING FOR BUSINESS

SIDNEY CALLIS

Chandos Publishing

Oxford · England

Chandos Publishing (Oxford) Limited
Chandos House
5 & 6 Steadys Lane
Stanton Harcourt
Oxford OX8 1RL
England
Tel: +44 (0) 1865 882727 Fax: +44 (0) 1865 884448
Email: sales@chandospublishing.com
www.chandospublishing.com

· ·

First published in Great Britain in 2001

ISBN 1 902375 74 2

© S. Callis, 2001

Printed by Biddles, Guildford, UK

For Bim

With love . . . for everything

Contents

Introduction

This is a book about writing – business writing. We all write all the time, from shopping lists to novels; our objective is to communicate in some way. But writing in a business context is special, because it has to do with our livelihood.

The main purpose of any writing is to communicate. To communicate we need words – plain simple words are best. Unfortunately many of us, when faced with having to do a piece of business writing, behave as if plain straightforward everyday language, which is a perfectly good means of communicating, ceases to exist. What takes over as soon as we pick up a pen or start to tap our keyboard is a weird mixture of what is imagined to be formal language; such writing is self-defeating and violates all the principles of effective communication.

The actual writing, which many people find difficult, probably represents the least problem – if you follow the method outlined in this book. The really important part of the job is the gathering and organisation of material. If there is insufficient material one tends to 'pad'. If there is too much, then one is overwhelmed by the task of getting it all in and the document becomes unwieldy and generally unreadable. For good business writing, choice of material and its proper organisation are equally, if not more, important than the writing itself.

So, observe the principle of:

Clarity – Simplicity – Brevity

If your writing is 'weird and wonderful' it will not be *clear*, neither will it be *simple* enough to understand easily. And if you 'pad', *brevity*, the essence of good writing, will be lost. These ideas are stressed, throughout this book in many ways – remember it.

The preparatory work, the thinking about the writing before even putting pen to paper, is considered at some length in this book. The more the writing is thought about and planned in advance, the easier it will be to actually write and the more successful in achieving its object it will be. Careful thought about: why you are writing; who is going to read it; what is to go in; what should be left out and how it is all to be arranged will be well rewarded when the time for actual writing comes. Too often, poor writing is the result of poor preparation. The document may be well written in good clear simple language but, because the facts are muddled and the conclusions suspect, it will fail in its purpose. The underlying lack of preparation will show through. Therefore, in order to communicate effectively, we stress the main principles of establishing purpose, identifying the readership, writing well and good preparation of the finished product.

There is no 'best way' to write. Anyone who has to do any sort of writing for their work – reports, surveys, proposals, memos, letters, whatever – will have evolved their own method. This book represents a distillation of experience, gathered over many years of professional writing and teaching others how to write effectively.

The chapters that follow may be used as a model both in language and layout for everything that good business writing should be. Observe the simple rules that are given and your business writing will be clear, concise and effective; and get things done!

About the author

Sidney Callis is a Chartered Accountant, who made a mid-life career change to become a management consultant, specialising not in finance, but in the absorbing field of human resource development. His passion for the English language prompted him to develop programmes to enable managers to improve their writing skills.

He has worked all over the world on numerous assignments for the World Bank, the Asian Development Bank, the EU and many other international bodies. He has run his own consultancy for the last fifteen years and continues to conduct respected and well-attended training seminars and workshops (especially in Business Writing) in South East Asia, Africa and the Caribbean.

He is chairman of the Blind Business Association Charitable Trust (BBACT) and a Council member of the Association of Business Executives, for whom he also edits *Business Executive* magazine.

The author may be contacted via the publishers.

CHAPTER 1

The preliminaries

'The time devoted to planning, cleaning, chopping, paring or trussing as the case may be, is not lost. The actual process of cooking is immensely facilitated, and success half-assured, if everything has been properly prepared beforehand.'

Mrs Beeton

1.1 Before you even begin to think about writing

1.1.1 Preliminaries

Before starting on any piece of business writing, you need to consider many things:

- First, remember that we are writing to communicate. All business writing needs a *purpose*. Communication is the presentation of facts, opinions and emotions to achieve an aim. Effective communication is targeted at a specific receiver: the *reader*.

- Then we need to assemble *material*. This involves allocating the various facts and ideas to appropriate groups and places.

- Now the *structure*. A good letter, report or proposal begins with a summary (like this one). It is easier to master a subject if you have an overall picture of what is involved. This is particularly true if complex relationships are being established. With the help of the summary, readers understand the material presented more easily.

- *Repetition* is an important aspect of effective communication. Put the main points over two or three times. We pay most attention to, and remember best, the beginning and the ending. Therefore, open and close strongly.

- Finally, consider how to split up the text. Present it easily and intelligibly; avoid continuous reading or excessive subdivision.

These factors – defining the purpose, identifying the reader, assembling the material and deciding the structure and division – are the preliminaries to good writing.

1.2 The five principles

There are five main principles of good writing:

GOOD WRITING FOR BUSINESS

1.   The *purpose* – why it is written.

2.   The *application* – how it is used.

3.   The *content* – what it says.

4.   The *expression* – how it says it.

5.   The *appearance* – what it looks like.

1.2.1 Principle 1: Purpose

This refers to why you are writing. You really should have something to say. Remember:

> Don't write if there is nothing to say.

Determine the purpose of your writing by asking and answering these questions:

•   What am I writing about?

•   Why am I writing it?

•   What will be the benefit to me of writing it?

Then ask the further question:

•   Is there a shorter, simpler, more effective way of achieving my purpose? (In other words – is this writing really necessary?)

Defining the purpose

The most important step in writing preparation is to define the purpose of the writing. You write to be read, and the purpose is defined by the effect the writing is intended to have on readers. They may, for example, read to acquire knowledge, authorise action, stop something, promote someone. The possibilities are endless, but it is absolutely essential that the writer has one particular purpose in mind from the start. Unless that purpose is constantly kept in mind while writing, the result will not achieve what is intended.

When the purpose has been properly identified, then there are clear answers to these questions:

• What am I writing about?

• How do I want to influence the reader?

• What do I want the reader to do?

• Is this writing the simplest, shortest and most effective way of achieving my purpose?

Finally, when all the questions have been answered in your mind, write down the purpose in one or two short sentences. This will crystallise the purpose and provide a focus for your writing to come.

What you should now be able to say is – 'as a result of reading this (letter, report, memorandum, etc.), the reader will . . .'

1.2.2 Principle 2: Application

This refers to how the writing is to be used, so make it appropriate to the circumstances

There are four main types of writing:

- for information – this deals with what has happened, or describes a state of affairs as in *historical* or *investigative* writing;

- for *explanation* – to explain changes (either actual or intended);

- for *persuasion* – here we make a complete case and include historical elements;

- to promote *discussion* – here we add the personal viewpoint in support for or against.

Each has a different use. The use must be defined and the appropriate type used.

Distinguish between the different types of writing. A style suitable for one purpose will not necessarily suit another. To achieve our purpose, we must decide in advance how the writing is to be used, and write it appropriately.

1.2.3 Principle 3: Content

This refers to what the writing says. Write it to suit the intended reader.

This is about tactics – how to get accepted and get the required action. Having defined the purpose – say, to recommend a production plan – we should then arrange the content to achieve maximum effect:

- put in items which will persuade the reader;

- leave out things which will not help to persuade the reader;

- arrange it in the best sequence (let the reader know the advantages *before* the problems);

- rearrange it – see what is finally included from the *reader's* point of view.

1.2.4 Principle 4: Expression

This refers to the writing style – how it says it. Say it as clearly as you can.

This may seem obvious! But there is much to say on this matter. Here we only emphasise the need for clarity.

> Write clearly, not cloudily.

1.2.5 Principle 5: Appearance

This refers to what it looks like. Make it look worth reading.

A scruffy-looking letter or report, however excellent the contents, only gets the attention it deserves – very little or none at all! All the paper in the reader's in-tray competes for a share of their time. An attractive presentation will gain the initial attention needed. After that, it will have to stand on its merits – but the initial impact is important.

The key features of effective presentation are:

- the right size, shape and quality of paper (A4 is standard, odd sizes irritate);

- the pages neatly bound, if appropriate, with a cover page and all fastened together securely;

- good layout with wide margins left and right, top and bottom;

- the typing and printing clean and well-aligned;

- numbered pages (it is amazing how often texts are presented without the pages numbered – even a two-page letter should have its second page numbered);

- no alterations, no errors and no spelling mistakes – in these days of word processors, PCs and photocopiers, there can be no excuse for poor proofreading.

All this means careful attention to detail.

1.3 Defining the reader

1.3.1 Who are they?

The purpose of the writing has been defined in various ways, depending on the effect it is intended to have. It is therefore important to identify the people at whom the writing is aimed before beginning to write.

Who the readers are can be found by answering these questions:

- What does the reader know about this subject?

- What does the reader know about the background of this subject?

- Does the reader have strong feelings on this subject?

1.3.2 Meeting the reader's needs

We must not be too clever, nor may we bore the reader with what he already knows. This is difficult when writing a report, for example, and there are several readers with different characteristics; in such a case one of the following courses of action can be used.

Write a full report but start with a short, clear summary

This format can be used when the most important reader is a specialist or has good background and actual knowledge. However some of his colleagues will not be concerned with technical details and will need only an outline summary.

Write a short, clear report with detailed appendices

This is appropriate when the important reader does not have detailed technical knowledge; his technical colleagues will read the appendices.

Write the report for the general reader, with
a full detailed version for the specialist

This format is not common except in very technical situations (e.g. computer specification).

1.3.3 Summary

Asking questions about the reader, knowing who the reader will be and writing for the reader are essential initial steps and are important in selecting and arranging the material. Once this is done we will begin to see the general form of the writing.

CHAPTER 2

Getting the facts, logic, conclusions and recommendations

'Now, what I want is Facts. Facts alone are wanted in Life.' (Mr Gradgrind)

Charles Dickens, *Hard Times*

2.1 Gathering the material

Having defined the purpose and identified the reader, you can start to assemble and arrange the material. This process will lead you to a satisfactory outline on the basis of which you will be able to write effectively.

In business writing facts will make up most of the material and are the most important part. Conclusions are drawn from them and recommendations based on them.

In any good writing the writer will have ensured that:

- all the facts are present – and correct;

- the conclusions are logical;

- the recommendations are sound.

2.2 Preparing the material

At this point the writer will have many questions.

- What is my material?

- Where do I find it?

- How much do I need?

- How shall I collect it?

- How do I arrange it?

- What order should it be in?

Attempting to deal with *all* these in an unstructured way will lead to confusion and wasted effort. The key to all preparation is to keep the purpose clearly in mind.

The first step is to get all your ideas on what could be included out of your head and onto paper. This can be done using a technique similar to 'mind mapping' combined with Ichikawa analysis – the 'pattern map'.

2.2.1 Using this technique

1. Write the main theme in the centre of a large sheet of paper (A3 is a good size).

2. Write down all the ideas and thoughts you have on the subject – start from the centre and branch out along chains of connecting ideas.

3. Let your mind be as free as possible. Do not restrict your thoughts by deciding where each point should go in a list – ideas should flow easily.

4. When you have got as much down as possible, circle related ideas and sections – use colour and link the points. It will look like a tangled ball of knitting wool!

5. Start to establish your order of priorities and organisation. Then plot them on a pattern map.

2.2.2 The pattern map

A pattern map on road transport problems might look like Figure 2.1.

Having completed the pattern map, most of your ideas will be on paper; also a pattern will begin to emerge. You can sort ideas into topics. Some ideas will be main headings for a number of other points.

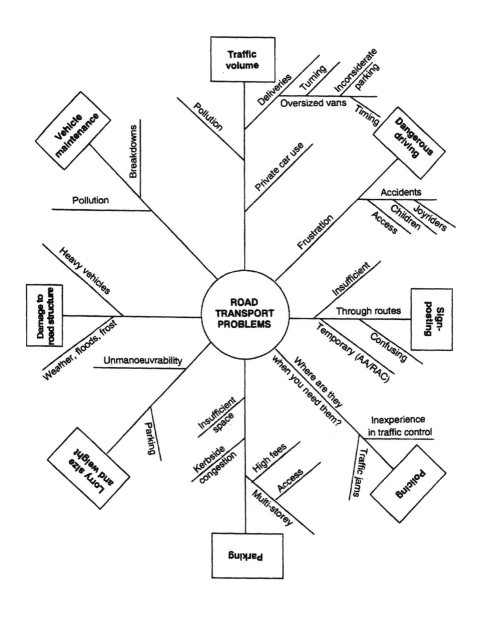

Figure 2.1 Example of a pattern map.

If you are writing a simple report or proposal, pattern maps can serve as the plan; collect the necessary evidence for each heading, select the essential headings and arrange them into a logical order.

2.2.3 *The column planner*

For more complex writing, or if you are writing over a long period, it helps to draw up a *column planner*, using the main ideas from the pattern map.

Draw up a matrix as indicated in Figure 2.2. Follow the procedure for each column from left to right across the page. In the left-hand column, 'topics to be covered', list the main headings from the pattern map.

You cannot begin to write until you understand the facts; you now have most of the facts, or at least know how to get them.

Collect the material under the selected topics in column 1; a good outline will begin to emerge. By using a pattern map and/or a column planner, you can make the important decisions on your writing.

Decide now on the conclusions and recommendations. Note them at the bottom of the plan.

- *Conclusions:* considered opinions – the writer's decisions based on assessment of the evidence.

- *Recommendations:* suggested action to resolve the problem and fulfil the purpose of the report.

Topics to be covered	Sources	Visuals	Material arrangement
This column answers: *'What do I need to know?'*	This column answers: *'Where do I get the information from?'*	This column answers: *'What visual materials do I need?'*	This column answers: *'In what order should I present my material?'*
Only collect material relevant to your terms of reference. Be guided by your principal reader. List the areas/items which you must include. These provide: • headings under which to gather the data; • section headings under which the data is ready sorted for writing. By covering only relevant areas you have made the first step in selecting your material.	List the sources of information at the side of each item. Sources will vary according to the subject. Do not forget: • People are important sources – the opinion of people may be very relevant; • Visits may be more relevant that second-hand information; • Look for earlier work on the subject or similar area.	Use only that which will help the reader's understanding. Always relate it to the text in question. Consider visual material now alongside each item in Column 1. Visual material can often replace words by doing a particular part of the job better. Decide now what is wanted: pictures, graphs, diagrams, etc.	Consider the *purpose* and the *reader*. These will indicate what are the most important factors. The nature of your subject will often determine the most logical order for your *material*. Focus points are at the beginning and the end – do not bury important factors in the middle. Number in this column the priority of items in Column 1.

Figure 2.2 The column planner.

2.2.4 Using the pattern map/column planner

Select from the complete findings only sufficient material essential to support the arguments leading to your conclusions and recommendations. Too much will obscure the point you wish to make and slow down the flow of your argument. Too little will present unfounded opinions and unjustified recommendations.

Try to find the right balance in each case. To get this balance: select on the basis of the purpose of the writing and the reader(s) it is intended for.

Arrange the order of presentation of each section, working from the pattern map or by using Column 4 of the planner. Arrangement of material within each separate item will be determined by the nature of the subject. The most logical order will usually be that which the reader can follow clearly.

Headings are signposts to the reader. Have a clear, logical, series of steps prepared before you start to write. At this stage you should have main and subheadings – this is your outline. Using it, decide in what order all the main sections of your material are to be placed.

2.2.5 The importance of outlining

Following compilation of the pattern map/column planner, outlining is the most important step in writing. It determines the logic of what you write and the quality of how you write it.

Planning the order of the ideas may be easy for very short letters and reports; intelligent structuring is much harder for a major writing job.

When you have trouble getting started, it is probably because you are trying to start 'correctly' – that means planning the proper order of the ideas in your mind before you start, which is almost impossible. You need a visual reference, such as the pattern map, to help organise your ideas. Outline before you write.

There is no one best way to arrange your ideas into a logical form. The method you use is a matter of your own personal work habits. Make sure, while arranging your ideas, that they are building into a structure that will help your reader. The outline should pass this five-point checklist:

- Is the subject obvious from the beginning?

- Is there a summary or overview very early?

- Is the information in a logical sequence?

- Is the emphasis of the various ideas balanced?

- Is it complete?

Outlining is the most important thinking area in your writing. But do not try to write at the same time – do not deal with the detailed words and sentences while dealing with the ideas.

Outlining needs time. Experienced writers often spend as much time outlining as writing. This may be more than you are used to, but it will mean less time spent later, when you actually begin writing.

2.3 The paragraph option

One of the main mistakes that anyone makes in writing is to try to write it all down from beginning to end. This can, perhaps, be done successfully for a fairly short piece of writing of no more than, say, 2,000 words, provided a good outline has been constructed first. For anything longer it is probably not feasible, nor necessary. This section describes the 'paragraph option'.

Any writing is built up of paragraphs. A paragraph is a block of sentences, preferably not more than 10 to 15 of them, extending for not more than 15 to 20 lines when in type. This means about 200 to 250 words in each. A paragraph expresses and explores a single idea. If you have more than one idea or statement of facts to express, start another paragraph.

The paragraphs can be written as you go along, after you have completed a bit of research upon which you have made some notes, or after an interview from which you have derived some facts. Write it then and there, or dictate it into a recorder for later transcription. Getting it down immediately in some manner is good discipline; it fixes the impression or idea or fact fast. It is also doing the writing. It may be necessary to write several paragraphs on one subject which is fine, but remember the length rule. A paragraph of one sentence is all right – it makes for dramatic emphasis. But a paragraph of a hundred sentences is not good. It is likely to be confused, boring (however fascinating the subject matter) and difficult to read.

Set paragraphs out on separate sheets of paper, double spaced with wide margins. If more than about two-thirds of a single A4 sheet of paper is covered, then you have written too much. Later, editing is going to be essential. When compiling a long report use different colours of paper; this helps to sort out subjects because you will have generated material from a wide range of sources and on a variety of topics – all of them (hopefully) relevant to the subject of the report. Thus, for example, put all paragraphs relating to finance on blue paper, marketing on yellow, and so on. Keep all the different subject paragraphs together with bulldog clips, numbering each page sequentially to start with (just so as not lose anything). Even if you are doing all your writing on a word processor, signal the different sections somehow, with distinct file numbers, so as to batch all the small segments together. Go through each batch and look for a logical sequence; remove any segments that are not relevant or that belong more appropriately in another section. Renumber and print out a fair draft in the sequence selected. Now most of the report is written.

Edit it, to harmonise writing style and to improve poor sentence construction and grammar. Then read it through carefully to ensure that the argument flows logically. However much editing is needed, the labour is still far less than if the whole thing had been written from scratch, using notes made during the investigation.

2.4 Facts, inferences and value judgements

There is a difference between these three forms of statement. A *statement of fact* is based on something you have observed and proved, in some way or other, or which someone else could also have observed.

A *statement of inference* sounds like a fact and could readily be accepted as such. However, what you really mean is 'I have just observed something and I infer (from behaviour, appearance or whatever) that something has or will occur'. This is what you think – but it is not a fact.

Finally, there is a *statement of value*. Here you make a judgement, for or against, good or bad, on what you have seen or heard. You form an opinion. There is often a danger in a value judgement as the underlying implication is that our own standards or judgements are the only true ones. The problem is that all three statements are written in the same way and, unless we differentiate them, the reader does not know which one we are using. This can be dangerous (and costly) if recommendations are based on opinions and not facts.

We cannot avoid drawing conclusions from facts but remember – a fact is not an inference, and an inference is not a value judgement. Keep them separate.

2.5 Conclusions

Conclusions are 'a logical deduction from information', or 'decisions based on assessment of the evidence'.

The conclusions section usually comes at the end of a report. Or it can be included at the end of each section with a summary at the end. The purpose is to make deductions based on the information presented. The conclusions answer the question 'so what?' after the information has been given. Do not include any new information.

In addition to making deductions based on the information, conclusions may also briefly summarise or highlight the main points. 'Jumping to conclusions' means making a deduction from insufficient evidence. Ensure that all the relevant information is given before making conclusions. Options may be expressed but must be logical; a lot of attention is needed here – poor logic is a very common fault.

Here is an example of a conclusion at the end of a report on choice of building sites:

CONCLUSION

Three sites were investigated which met all the criteria to some degree. Site 1 was much the cheapest in cost. There was no significant difference on the question of providing building services. Site 2 was marginally more convenient for rail and motorway access. However, Site 3 was the only one within a reasonable distance of a suitable workforce pool. Without this the project is not viable. The cost of building at Site 1 would outweigh the initially lower cost of purchasing the land.

No one site is clearly superior on all criteria; the decision must be the best compromise.

The conclusion must:

- be short;

- not contain any information which has not already been given;

- summarise, if at all, only the main points;

- make logical deductions from the information given.

2.5.1 Getting to logical conclusions

A logical conclusion is arrived at by a number of steps, arranged so that one step leads to another. However, there are often errors in the logic chain.

Here are the five most frequent faults of logic:

Too few steps in the reasoning sequence

It is important to get into the reader's mind to find out how familiar he is with the argument. The writer may know all the steps, but failure to explain the steps will cause loss of understanding.

Too many steps in the reasoning sequence

Conversely, to explain painstakingly all the steps to a reader who knows them shows a failure to understand the reader. This irritates and hampers communication.

Steps out of sequence

This can cause the writing to be labelled 'confusing'. It throws doubt on the conclusions and recommendations and also on the writer's ability and authority.

Conclusions which are unjustified

Generalising from the particulars is an easy error to make. It quickly discredits the writer in the mind of the reader.

Do not assume that:

- what has happened in the short term will also occur in the long term;

- what has happened in one place is true of other places;

- how a few people behave is characteristic of all the people involved.

Occasionally it is necessary to generalise from the particular, for example when the missing facts cannot be obtained. In such circumstances specifically state the generalisation made to ensure that the reader is aware of it. Always take the reader into your confidence. Play fair and explain; don't bluff – you will be found out.

Emotional writing

Emotion and reason do not go well together. Emotion, the expression of strong feelings, has a vital place in spoken communication where emotion rather than logic is the most effective tool of persuasion. However, written material should rely on logical reasoning and avoid emotional emphasis. We are not,

---

after all, writing a novel. Emotion in business writing kills its objectivity and damages a good case.

2.5.2 How to achieve logic

To achieve a logical arrangement of writing material it is helpful to follow these six steps:

Write down the main points

For a short report, a single page of paragraph headings is probably sufficient, plus a list of any tables or diagrams which may be necessary. For a longer document, use a separate page for each main section and make a short synopsis of its contents.

Select the necessary points

The key question is: 'Does the reader need this point to ensure understanding?' Cut out the remainder.

Group related points together

This requires a decision on the basis of the groups and this depends on the relationships to be established. Often, groupings and selection occur together, because grouping may partly determine selection.

Insert relevant headings

At this stage, headings should be put in between the groups and within them. Headings guide the reader, act as a quick introduction to the various parts and assist the author. Headings, when written out together, should form a clear synopsis of the document.

Headings should be informative but not too long: 'Comparison of performance with and without additives' is better than simply 'Comparison'. You will note in this book that the headings are generally short but sufficiently explanatory. Six or seven words is the maximum that should be used.

Group points in logical order

The various points within each group now need to be put in the right order; the logical sequence which presents the story to the reader most effectively. It is also important that the last point of each group rounds it off properly, and the first point in the next group leads the reader into the new idea.

Checking the logic

Few people can read their own work and find all the faults in their writing. Most serious books contain a note of thanks, often to several people, for 'reading the manuscript'.

This is a good idea. If possible get someone to read what you have written critically and discuss it with you. It will be significantly better if the writing and logic are checked and faults corrected before presentation.

Never 'rush into print'. Allow at least two or three days 'meditation time' after you have completed the first draft. Then, when the editing process starts, you can look at your work much more objectively and thus improve it greatly.

2.6 Recommendations

A report is often written so that recommendations can be made. This is especially true when persuasion and discussion have to take place. Management need information on which to base decisions.

A recommendation is a suggested course of action proposed to be taken, arising from the information and arguments set out. Each recommendation, and the reason for it, needs to be dealt with separately and fully.

Remember the difference between conclusions and recommendations. Many people will look at the same problem and often reach the same conclusions from the evidence, but by differing routes. However, the recommendations they make could vary widely, and legitimately so. Your own recommendations, supported by well-argued conclusions, need to be defended with conviction. If you have to hesitate about a recommendation – don't make it. Re-examine your arguments before committing yourself and your readers to what could be a costly mistake.

Recommendations made must be stated clearly and objectively. They must be practical and realistic. Wherever relevant, they should indicate that the recommendation has been arrived at with the agreement of the people affected by the proposals. The recommendations are generally the most important part of a report the value of which is enhanced by their soundness. However, the reverse is true also.

The following principles are important:

- Every major conclusion needs to be matched by a recommendation (even if it is a recommendation to do nothing).

- Every recommendation must be preceded by facts and conclusions; these will have prepared the reader for the recommendation.

2.6.1 Summary of recommendations

It is often useful to have a summary of recommendations very near the beginning, as part of the opening summary.

- Express the recommendations clearly and briefly.

- Base the recommendations on the information given . . .

- . . . and on the deductions made in the conclusion.

- Start with: 'It is recommended that . . .'

The aim is to enable the reader to grasp the subject matter easily, and the document should be read on the basis of justifying the recommendations. Each summary recommendation should state the facts simply and be written briefly and clearly. There must be no doubt at all about the recommendation being made.

2.7 Structure

The sequence of any writing, i.e. the parts of which it is composed, must be logical.

The actual headings and subheadings that will appear will be varied, but will all fall within these groupings:

- Introduction

- Information collected ('findings')

- Analysis of the information ('conclusions')

- Recommendations.

In the 'findings', it is essential that the headings show a logical progression which enables the reader to find a clear path through the document.

Whatever system of structuring is used, logic and the achievement of a clear flow of information to positively support the argument is the objective.

2.7.1 Introduction

The opening of any piece of business writing should give the reader a good idea of what is to come.

Title

If you are writing a report or other important document, a good title is essential. It should be short and contain the message of the report. This helps to start the reader's understanding.

Foreword

A brief foreword states what the writing is about and why it has been written – three or four lines at the very most.

Contents list

A contents list is essential even if there are only a few pages. It should have headings and subheadings. Do not list headings which do not appear or omit ones which do as the reader will be confused. Include the page number of each heading, a schedule of tables within the text and appendices with contents. A contents list can also serve as an index. However, if more detailed referencing is required, then an index should be placed at the end of the document.

Terms of reference

The terms of reference should be included but a summary is sufficient. Include the terms of reference in an appendix which can be referred to. The terms of reference will establish the purpose of the current investigation and outline the background of the situation or problem and any previous attempts at a solution.

Methodology

It is often useful to include a section on the methodology used, e.g.:

• what statistical analysis and sampling was used;

• who was interviewed, why and when;

• what desk and field research was done;

• what authorities were consulted;

• and so on.

This gives added credibility to the findings.

2.7.2 Summary

The summary is written last. It is a self-contained précis of the document. It must cover every main point, ideally giving two or three sentences to each, including the recommendations. It contains nothing which is not already included. Brevity is very important – do not rewrite your report for the summary!

2.7.3 Information collected (findings)

The findings should be classified into appropriate categories. It is best to arrange the material in a series of logical steps so as to lead the reader from what he knows to your view of the subject.

The findings should be identified by informative headings and subheadings which provide a quick logical overview to the flow of the material.

Analysis and conclusions

The analysis is a discussion of the findings. Many ideas and themes will have been raised by the findings which the discussion then draws together.

Do not introduce fresh evidence at this stage. If new relevant material is found, even if it is rather late, insert it in the correct place in the findings.

The analysis leads to conclusions which should be arranged in order of importance, and be expressed clearly, briefly and precisely.

Recommendations

Recommendations are generally the most important part of a report – often the real reason it is written. They should be brief, stated in order of importance, sound and acceptable.

2.7.4 Appendices

Never overload any document with material which can be put in an appendix.

Never put into an appendix irrelevant information – everything in the appendix must be necessary. There is always severe temptation to save material which is interesting, or on which you have taken a great deal of trouble. Resist the temptation and be ruthless when you come to editing – 'if in doubt, throw it out'.

The criteria for keeping material in the main text or placing it in an appendix are:

• Is it necessary for my reader to study these facts now?

• Or can they take them on trust for the moment and get on with the story?

• Will this material distract the reader at the present time?

This particularly applies to complex tables, charts, etc. which need careful study. Refer the reader to the relevant appendix, and let them get on with reading.

2.8 Numbering and classifying

How numbering and classifying is dealt with depends on two factors: the length of the document and the need for internal referencing. Some form of numbering is necessary to identify the parts of a long document if frequent reference to other parts is needed. For both internal referencing and for the reader, page numbers are absolutely essential. This applies even to a two-page letter.

Use text headings which are numbered; the decimal system used in this book is simple and logical. Begin by numbering each chapter, e.g. 2. The various sections of chapter 2 are then numbered 2.1, 2.2, etc. The subsections are numbered 2.1.1, 2.1.2 etc.

Do not go into double figures in any decimal numbering. It is better to rearrange the material.

For smaller identifications within a sub-subsection, we prefer to use a small roman number.

All this is necessary for a lengthy report to ensure ease of access and reference. Short documents or a book can safely be accessed using a less elaborate schematic.

2.9 Division and numbering

There are no hard and fast rules as to how the division into sections and subsections etc. and the layout is achieved. This will depend on your own taste or the house style. Layout should aim for maximum clarity; the style suggested here is clear, tasteful and relevant for business reports. Whatever style is used, it should be consistent throughout.

2.9.1 Four divisions

There are four divisions for the text. How they are formatted on the page is very much dependent on the house style. These divisions, with their headings, are as follows:

- The main subdivision is into chapters. For instance, the chapters in this book start:

  1 The preliminaries

  2 Getting the facts

- Headings are set to the left. They can be set out in different typefaces and sizes, or they may be typed in italic capitals and underlined.

- The next division is into sections. For example, the main headings in this chapter are:

  2.1 Gathering the material

  2.2 Preparing the material

  2.3 The paragraph option

  etc.

Main section headings may be smaller capitals, set to the left margin. Or the style of layout can be adapted to suit your needs. The text of sections is typed to full margins left and right.

- The next division is into subsections. You are now reading subsection 2.9.1 headed 'Four divisions'.

  Subsections are typed with an additional margin to the left. Subsections can have headings if required. These should be in small capitals or in a different typeface, and set either on the same line as the text or just above the first text line.

- The final division is into sub-subsections. This final division can be lettered, or small roman numerals can be used. We could possibly have made each of the bullet points into sub-subsections, but this would have been clumsy. Sub-subsections have an additional margin at the left, but not at the right. They do not normally have headings.

Do not subdivide still further – rearrange the material instead. To have more divisions confuses the reader and makes for a scrappy final appearance. Good layout assists readability and helps get your document accepted. Adapt these ideas to the needs of your presentation. Rearrange and create more chapters. This will make it easier for the reader to absorb, because information is being presented in small bite-sized chunks, not in tortuous lengthy indigestible blocks.

CHAPTER 3

Writing clearly and measuring writing

'It is wise not to begin to write until you are quite certain what you want to say.'

Sir Ernest Gowers, *The Complete Plain Words*

3.1 Writing clearly

3.1.1 Clear, familiar words

Language is a tool, a means to an end, not an end in itself. When using words, especially in a business context, look for precision and ease of understanding. Choose words that convey what you mean accurately and which are familiar to the reader. Never use an unfamiliar word when you can say precisely the same thing with a familiar one. Don't increase the communication gap between the writer and the reader.

If you compare a random list of short words with a random list of long words, many more of the short words will be familiar to you. There are exceptions, but short words tend to be easier to read and understand than long words.

You will have to use some long words. Shortness is no guarantee of precision. Precision is whether the words exactly convey the writer's intended meaning. Occasionally you may choose to use long words or phrases, even though shorter ones are available to say the same thing. For example, the long phrase may have some special professional meaning such as 'in our opinion' which means the same as 'we think', but 'in our opinion' has some special meaning.

3.1.2 Keep most sentences short and simple

Good writing keeps sentence length to an average of between 15 and 20 words. But mix them up. Let the size and shape of the idea dictate the size and shape of the sentence. Remember: the shorter the sentence, the harder it hits.

Good writing is also simple. This means one major idea to a sentence. If sentences get very long, they will contain more than one major idea. There is then a risk of grammatical error, and the reader may not get the meaning intended. A good sentence can be quite long. But writing long sentences well requires great writing skill. Keeping the grammar correct and the ideas untangled is difficult work.

Grammatically correct does not necessarily mean clear. Long sentences often obscure the ideas they contain. Like difficult words, they increase communication difficulties between writer and reader. Separate long sentences into several shorter ones; you will then be able to say what you want to say, clearly and accurately. This will speed up your writing. Dividing one long sentence into two or more short ones clarifies difficult subject matter. Try to cut long compound sentences (two independent clauses, one after the other but separated by a comma and connecting word instead of a full stop). Chop the long sentence into two. Change the comma to a full stop and use a capital letter to begin the second half. It may be necessary to change a few words to correct the grammar after the chop. This is a quick and easy way to improve your writing.

One major idea to a sentence does not mean ruling out subordinate clauses. But these should contain less important ideas. When there are two major ideas in one grammatical structure, one of them loses impact. It may get passed over, or the ideas may share emphasis equally and both fail to get proper attention from the reader.

The more full stops writing contains, the better it will be. But do not shorten sentences too much. This will make the writing sound choppy. If writing averages between 15 and 20 words per sentence, it will flow smoothly. Put in the occasional sentence of just a few words, as we have done here. This will lighten your writing greatly.

Good writing should be as brief as possible. Brevity is desirable, but clarity is more important. Readers mentally measure writing by how long it takes to read. Clear writing takes less time to read. To the busy reader brevity is a matter of clarity – and good organisation – more than of number of words or pages.

The characteristics that make writing clear also make it brief. But do not be too brief or some serious flaws may develop; you may leave out important information, and you may sound blunt or rude.

3.1.3 Prefer active voice verbs; avoid passives

It is occasionally necessary to use the passive voice verb. But its tone is usually stilted, dull and often imprecise.

The basic sentence structure in the English language is:

Subject . . . transitive verb . . . direct object.

This is the 'active voice' because the subject performs some action on the object. For example:

The manager	prepared	the schedule.
(subject)	(transitive verb)	(direct object)
The principal	signed	the report.

In the passive voice, these examples will read:

The schedule	was prepared	by the manager.
(subject)	(intransitive verb)	(indirect object)
The report	was signed	by the principal.

In sentences with passive voice verbs the subject and object change places and roles. The subject receives the action instead of performing it. Thus this structure is 'passive'. The passive voice is rarely stimulating to the reader. Sentences with active verbs have a more interesting tone; the reader is encouraged to go on reading.

Occasionally you may wish to emphasise the action without identifying the source. In such circumstances use the passive. But the passive can leave gaps in the ideas and the writer may unwittingly omit useful information. Grammatically, the passive sentence does not need an object. Its object becomes an indirect object (of the preposition 'by'), which is not a necessary part of the sentence. The writer may leave out the whole prepositional phrase. The sentences would then look like this:

The schedule was prepared.

The report was signed.

If we drop the indirect object the reader cannot tell who performed the action in these examples, and who performed the action may be important for the reader to fully understand.

Avoid the passive for written instructions. Do not write: 'The statement must be updated every three months'. It is unclear and may not get done if there is any question about who must do it. Write: 'You (or whoever else) must update the statement every three months'. Active voice verbs tell who is responsible for what much more clearly than passive voice verbs.

To turn a passive sentence active, ask yourself:

'BY WHOM?'

The answer to that question should be the subject.

The passive is not always a past tense, although they can sound alike. Do not be confused on this point. Passives occur in all verb tenses – and are equally poor in all. Try to avoid the passive wherever possible.

3.1.4 Get people into your writing

Many people think that business writing must be impersonal. Occasional reference to oneself is perfectly acceptable, even in the most dignified writing. But before you write 'I', ask yourself if 'we' might be more appropriate. This is when you are writing about something done for the company. Don't overdo it, and do not bring people into your writing unnecessarily, or deliberately block them out. Name departments, companies, government agencies or other organisations that may be part of what you are writing about; refer to them if it seems appropriate.

Referring to the people involved will make your writing sound more courteous. More importantly, the writing will be clearer and more precise.

3.1.5 Use a conversational style

Professional writers use conversational style as a guide. It is especially useful when writing difficult passages. When you are having trouble finding the right words, ask yourself: 'How would I say this to my reader if we were face to face?' Table 3.1 shows some examples.

But take care, we are all a bit careless in conversation. We can be, because the listener will ignore or not notice small mistakes. But the reader is less likely to ignore them. Therefore the writer must be more careful than the talker to be grammatically correct.

We are not suggesting that you be 'breezy' or use slang in your writing. Good writing should be grammatically correct but not stilted. In most of your business writing you will want to sound formal. But do not confuse formality with stilted, obscure, complicated writing. You can be formal and still express yourself clearly and simply.

Table 3.1 Examples of the conversational style

Stiff:	'It is the responsibility of supervisors to maintain surveillance over operating departments' performance methods and routines to ensure compliance with approved standard procedures.'
Conversational:	'Supervisors must make sure workers follow standard procedures.'
Stiff:	'It was anticipated that the causes of the shortages could be identified, with the objective that repetition of the same errors could be avoided in the future.'
Conversational:	'We hoped to learn what caused the shortages, to help prevent them in the future.'

3.1.6 Get all the information before writing

To write clearly you must have confidence in your ideas. You cannot write an idea clearly until you have thought it out clearly. And you cannot think it out clearly until you have all the information necessary to do so. Gathering all the information in advance will encourage clarity by giving you confidence that your ideas will be impressive.

Take notes from the beginning of any project. But do not try to write these notes as a finished product. Remember the paragraph option (see section 2.3). Use your paragraphs to develop clear ideas. Do not start the final writing, however, until you have all the information you need for the clear thinking that clear writing demands.

You do not have to complete the entire project before you write anything. Most projects can be divided into parts that stand alone. It is possible to complete first drafts of major sections without the entire job being finished. But ensure, in your editing, that all the sections blend into a harmonious whole.

3.2 Measuring readability

Various formulas have been devised to measure reading workload. These formulas may seem to oversimplify the task of measuring readability, but they are useful, especially to people interested in improving their writing skills.

3.2.1 Readability

We have all been faced with unreadable books and reports, which demand so great an effort from the reader that comprehension is lost. Many researchers have analysed bad writing to determine how it differs from good writing. To quote just two examples:

- In 1947, in *Politics and the English Language*, George Orwell listed six rules 'that one can rely on when instinct fails'.

- In 1968, in *The Technique of Clear Writing*, Robert Gunning (originator of the Fog Index) set out 10 principles of clear writing.

Their two lists have much in common. They found that readable writing has some or all of the features shown in Table 3.2. We could add a few more items, such as:

- no ambiguities;

- sufficient personal references;

- interesting constructions;

- no clichés.

There are so many terrible things you can do to make your writing unreadable! Ignore any of the items above and you are well on the way to unreadable writing. Unfortunately many writers do disregard these principles of clear writing.

3.2.2 Readability index

There are two key factors which affect the readability of a piece of writing:

- the number of words in a sentence;

- the number of difficult or unusual words used.

Table 3.2 Features of readable writing

Gunning	Orwell
Keep sentences short.	
Prefer the simple to the complex.	
Prefer the familiar word.	Never use a foreign phrase, a scientific word or a jargon word if you can find an everyday English equivalent.
Avoid unnecessary words.	If it is possible to cut a word out, always cut it out.
Put action in your verbs.	Never use the passive where you can use the active.
Write like you talk.	
Use terms your reader can picture.	
Tie in with your reader's experience.	
Make full use of variety.	
Write to express, not impress.	Never use a long word when a short one will do.
	Never use a metaphor, simile or figure of speech which you are used to seeing in print.
	Break any of these rules rather than say anything altogether barbarous.

Rudolf Flesch, in his book *The Art of Readable Writing*, gave the following relationship between average sentence length and understanding:

If a sentence contains on average:	*It will be understood on first reading by:*
30 words or more	5% of readers.
17–19 words	75% of readers.
7 words or less	95% of readers.

Therefore aim for an average of about 20 words to a sentence. But maintain interest – variety of length is more important than the average. A lot of very short sentences will make the writing jerky.

The Flesch readability index takes into account both sentence length and the number of difficult words used.

3.2.3 Using the Clarity Index method

To measure readability using the Clarity Index, follow these steps:

1. Select a sample passage of writing that you wish to index. It should be not less that 100 or more than 400 words. For convenience, work with a sample of about 200–300 words. If you want more words, choose a couple of samples each of about 200 words from two sections of the text.

2. Calculate the average number of words per sentence in the sample passage by counting the total words then the number of sentences. Divide total words by total sentences (Factor 'W').

3. Calculate the percentage of long words, or 'polysyllables', in the passage. (Count as a polysyllable any word of three or more syllables. Exclude proper nouns, i.e. capitalised names of people, places, companies or products). Divide the number of long words by the total words in the chosen text to get the percentage (Factor 'S').

4. Add the results of Steps 2 and 3. The result is the Clarity Index for the passage. The Clarity Index for section 3.2.3 so far is around 22. There are about 167 words and 13 sentences, so Factor W = 13 (there is no need to be exact to three decimal places!). There are some 14 polysyllabic words, thus the percentage, Factor S, is about 9. So:

$$W (13) + S (9) = 22$$

This is quite low, but it is a simple and easy to understand calculation.

Special cases

- *Numbers.* When counting words per sentence, count all numbers as words. For example, 2001 is counted as one word. When calculating percentage of polysyllables, count numbers as polysyllables if they contain five or more digits.

- *Dates.* Count parts of a date (day, month and year) as separate words.

- *Hyphenated words.* When counting words per sentence, count all the parts as one word. When counting syllables, do not add all of the syllables of the hyphenated word; count it as a polysyllable only if one (or more) of the parts has over two syllables.

- *Verb forms.* Those ending with 'ed' and 'es' do not count as an extra syllable.

- *Lists.* If several pieces of information are separately numbered, and so can be read separately, count them as separate sentences, even though they may be grammatically one sentence.

- *Tables.* Do not include these. The Clarity Index applies only to text.

3.2.4 What are the desirable limits?

For writing that is easy to read but not overly simple, the Clarity Index should be between 30 and 35. But anything between 25 and 40 is acceptable. At 45 the writing is difficult to read. At 50, it is usually very hard to understand in sustained reading. Anything under 20 may be perfectly clear, yet might risk offending the reader by sounding too simple.

Writing at various levels

Professional people often disagree on levels of writing. Some feel they need not be concerned about sentence length or word difficulty if the reader is technically trained in the subject matter. Therefore knowing as much as possible about the reader(s) is essential.

Certainly, technically trained readers will have less difficulty understanding complex material in their fields than untrained readers. But you cannot predict the energy any particular reader may need to spend to fully understand the message. The reading audience will include people with different levels of technical understanding. So it is probably best to keep the Clarity Index at a moderately low level to ensure reader understanding.

Any combination of sentence length and vocabulary totalling between 30 and 35 will be a reasonable workload level. Use 35 as a target index, then analyse the two numbers that get you there.

For example, in a passage of your own writing, you might count 15 words per sentence and 20 per cent polysyllables. Or 22 words per sentence and 13 polysyllables. Both would be at a readable word/sentence workload of 35, but any mix about 35 will be a satisfactory workload for your reader.

If a particular subject demands a heavy vocabulary, simply compensate by shortening sentences. Manipulate the factors in the reader's workload in this way and it will make a great difference to whether they understand your ideas easily.

3.2.5 Use any readability formula with caution

The Clarity Index only gives a measure of the reader's workload based on sentence length. It cannot measure whether the ideas progress logically from sentence to sentence. It provides a reasonable measure of the familiarity of the vocabulary, but even on this point cannot be accurate. The Index cannot measure whether the most precise word has been used, or whether the word is familiar or not.

With all readability formulas a low score is no guarantee of good writing. But a high score is a strong indication of over-complex writing. If you accept that limitation, you will have kept the vocabulary and sentence workload reasonable for the reader.

CHAPTER 4

Writing

'The difficulty is not to write, but to write what you mean, not to affect your reader but to affect him precisely as you wish.'

Robert Louis Stevenson

4.1 Introduction

There are few rules to tell anyone how to write. All we can do is give some advice. Probably the most helpful is to get on with it, without interruption or delay; get all the facts and ideas on paper. At this stage do not get sidetracked into rewriting. Not many letters or reports are perfect at the first attempt. Often as much time will need to be spent on revision as on the first draft. So do not worry about getting it right. If you are communicating in writing it needs to be written!

One of our five principles is the need to pay attention to expression – say it as clearly as you can. We will try to give some advice on style.

4.2 Order of writing

Once you have decided the right structure to meet the readers' needs, you may be tempted to start to write in that sequence. That is not the best order in which to do the writing. It is probably better to start with the detail and follow the line of thinking through, from the problem to the solution.

4.2.1 Suggested writing sequence

1. *Main sections.* Work from the problem, through the methods and findings, to a discussion of those findings. Within the main sections, you can piece together your material, using the paragraph option, as we have suggested. There is no need for rigid scheduling – fit the pieces in their slots as you write them; shift them about to get the most clear and logical sequence.

2. *Conclusions.* Summarise the key points from the main sections.

3. *Recommendations.* These arise directly from the conclusions.

4. *Appendices.* Include here all the detailed data not needed in the main sections (although some appendices may have been created while writing the main sections).

5. *Preliminaries.* These comprise the miscellaneous items that will introduce the report: table of contents; purpose; terms of reference; methodology; background and so on.

6. *Summary.* This section can only be written when everything else is complete.

4.3 Getting started

Many people find it difficult to get started on a piece of writing. When faced with a blank sheet of paper, even the most experienced writers can get a mental block.

Here are five ideas to help you get started:

- *Let your rough ideas take form in your mind.* Often we cannot get started because the thoughts we want to express are not clear in our own mind. Give yourself time to let your ideas 'simmer', but don't use this as an excuse to keep putting off writing.

- *Talk to other people about your ideas.* Discussing your thoughts and plans will often bring out new ideas, and will help you form your own ideas more clearly.

- *Write as you think.* It is difficult to start writing in a clearly structured way. To get started, just 'dump' all your thoughts down on paper either in a totally unstructured way or use the pattern map technique. The important thing is to keep the pen moving and the ideas flowing freely. Offload your thoughts in brief note form so there is not too much to write. Then, go over what you have down on paper. Use it to create an ordered and logical outline structure.

- *Write visually.* It may be easier to put your thoughts down in the form of diagrams such as flowcharts, sketches or 'mind maps'. Words are not the only way to get your ideas on paper. As with the previous technique, go back over your 'visuals' and use them to create an ordered outline structure of what you plan to write.

- *Write – don't edit.* Grammar, punctuation and spelling are initially not important. Getting ideas down on paper is the first step. Tidy up the writing later.

Use any or all of these ideas. Choose those that best suit what you have to write, your own work style and – most important – the one that gets you started on the writing.

4.4 Style

All writing should be readable and interesting, and communicate its message clearly and unambiguously. Meet these aims by writing in a good, clear style.

There are no hard and fast rules – rules are a substitute for the thought which is essential for improving a writer's style. The most common fault is attempting to impress by style, rather than expressing what you want to say.

Lee Iacocca, the former Chief Executive of Chrysler, was definitely against trying to impress by style. There is a paragraph in his autobiography, which is particularly apt; he says:

> 'Say it in English, and keep it short. I once read a 15-page paper that was tough to understand. I called in the author and asked him to explain what was in the tome he had written. He did it in two minutes flat. He identified what we were doing wrong, what we could do to fix it, and what he recommended. When he finished I asked him why he didn't write in the paper the way he'd just said it to me. He didn't have an answer. All he said was: "I was taught that way".'

Iacocca's wisdom is a guide to all writers: essentially – keep it simple, keep it short. We can train ourselves away from the outmoded fashions of writing that we were schooled into. We can learn to write colloquially and communicate effectively.

4.4.1 Style in report writing

In this section we are talking about style in report writing, but it is equally applicable to any business writing.

Style is not some gloss of fancy language added to a plain statement of fact. All language has a style created by the words we choose, and the way we structure those words into a sentence.

Main styles of writing

There are three main styles that range from the formal, through the friendly to the familiar. The range has a continuous structure, but it can be divided into three broad classifications:

Formal: The newly inaugurated copying system has enjoyed a most favourable reception.

Friendly: Our new copying system has become really popular with the departments that use it.

Familiar: It's fab to see the new copying system going down such a treat.

The more formal the style, the more likely we are to use less familiar words and less simple verb forms – such as the passive voice.

At the other extreme, the familiar style will drop into using slang words and, possibly, phrases in place of complete sentences.

Style for reports

The choice of style for reports will be in the friendly to formal range. Familiar is not usually suitable. How formal or friendly you make the writing is a matter of individual preference, organisational custom and – most importantly – the feelings and expectations of your reader(s). But do not let out-of-date assumptions prejudice your views on your readers' expectations.

Reports were traditionally written in a very formal style: no personal pronouns; heavy use of the passive voice; long words rather than short ones. Business today, however, is carried out in a different social climate; readers tend to prefer shorter, more easily readable reports. Achieve this by using the friendly style of writing.

Aim for a style that is simple, human and precise. To help you achieve this:

- Keep a picture of your main reader in mind – write as if to the individual. This will keep a human touch in what you say.

- If you have problems getting away from the traditional formal report writing style, gaze into space. Then, picture your reader(s) in your mind; think what you would say to them if they were there, with you. Then, write it down. You may have to edit what you have written because of the limitations of the written word, but you will probably have expressed your thoughts in a clear and simple way (see the comments by Lee Iacocca above).

- Do not worry about style while you are writing. Say what you want to say, then sort out the way you have said it when you review what you have written.

4.5 Avoid the MILI principle: how to write clearly, simply and specifically

4.5.1 The MILI principle

Many people adopt the MILI principle when they start to put words together into phrases and sentences to:

Make It Look Important

The result is that, because of the padding to bulk the writing up with unnecessary words and phrases, the reader has difficulty understanding the message. So write clearly, simply and specifically.

Here are some common pitfalls to avoid:

- superfluous words

- pompous phrases

- vague, abstract words and phrases

- 'hedging'

- the proximity rule

- misuse of pronouns

- words with several meanings

- double negatives.

Superfluous words

It is easy to add second words that add nothing and repeat a meaning already given, for example:

- 'staff of suitable *calibre* (Overemphasis and confusion of
  and *quality*'   meaning.)

- 'I *personally* believe...' (Who else believes?)

Another common fault is unnecessary adjectives and adverbs:

- *true* facts   (If it *is* a fact it is true.)

- *actively* investigate   (Can you investigate passively?)

- *active* consideration   (Can you consider passively?)

- *quite* unique   ('Unique' means the only one.)

- *absolutely* impossible   ('Impossibility' is absolute.)

- an *unfilled* vacancy   (A vacancy *is* something unfilled!)

- I *would* suggest   (If you mean it, why be tentative?)

- *completely* fatal   (Can something be half fatal?)

The list is endless! Ruthlessly edit these banalities out of your writing.

Pompous phrases

This form of traditional, pointless jargon is described by the Oxford Concise Dictionary as 'barbarous or debased language'. Many of the phrases are clichés that we use unthinkingly:

- 'further to the above' (referring to a heading)

- 'the aforementioned'

- 'at this moment in time'

- 'at the end of the day'

- 'in the not too distant future'

- 'a substantial proportion'

- 'for the reason that'

- 'taking into consideration'

Again, seek out these and similar ghastly phrases and get them out of your writing.

Vague, abstract words and phrases

Using long-winded phrases leads to vagueness. Be specific in your writing. Do not write:

It was suggested that consideration be given to the possibility of improvement in our facilities for conferences with the object of elimination of noise and provision of adequate ventilation.

if you can write:

We need a better place to meet. This room is noisy and hot.

Use concrete rather than abstract words: they are more easily understandable. A concrete word is something you can see or feel. For example:

- chair

- desk

- computer.

An abstract word is *not* something you can see or feel. They generally represent concepts (an abstract word itself!). For example:

- communication

- democracy

- memory

- facility.

Try to choose words which convey precise ideas to your readers, for example:

Do not write:	if you can write:
transport facilities	trains, cars, lorries
educational amenities	schools, colleges
communication	e-mail, letter, phone call
research facilities	chemistry laboratory
computing facilities	computers
worker on a temporary basis	temporary staff
in the engineering field	in engineering
the human factor	people

The more directly you express yourself the happier your reader will be.

'Hedging'

Words such as 'perhaps', 'probably', 'comparatively', etc. are used by writers to avoid committing themselves. If that is your deliberate intention then all right.

However, if it is not intended, it destroys conviction. Where these words carry such implications, avoid them.

Also avoid vague adjectives and adverbs, such as 'significant', 'appreciable', 'substantial', 'soon'. Use specific figures, dates, times and so on.

Avoid words that sit on the fence and 'hedge' the meaning until it has no meaning. In the example below, the *italicised* words 'hedge':

> Additional evidence *suggests* that the difference in the midrange of the curves *may possibly indicate* a curve form that our *hypothesis may not adequately encompass.*

Are you any wiser!

The proximity rule

Keep modifying words or phrases close to the word or phrase they modify, otherwise your meaning will be uncertain. For example:

> *A discussion was held on overtime working in the office.*

What went on in the office – the discussion or the overtime working? Or was the discussion held while the staff were on overtime? Make the meaning quite clear; rewrite the sentence – even if it becomes a bit longer – and use punctuation. For example:

> *A discussion, on overtime working, was held in the office.*

Do not write that

> *The work area needs cleaning badly.*

when you mean

The work area badly needs cleaning.

Misplaced modifiers can also be amusing (but may make you look rather foolish):

We saw a man on a horse with a wooden leg.

The fire was extinguished before any damage was done by the fire brigade.

He told her that he wanted to marry her frequently.

Misuse of pronouns

Be careful not to use a pronoun when you have already used two nouns in that sentence – or sometimes in a preceding sentence. For example:

Mary told Susan she was being promoted.

Who was being promoted?

The car collided with the van at the crossroads. It had to be towed away quickly to avoid a traffic jam.

What had to be towed away?

Words with several meanings

Many words that have two (or more) meanings may leave the reader in doubt about your message. For example:

We *dispense* with accuracy.

John is *aggressive*.

It is *practically* done.

If you are unsure of a word that you feel/know has more than one meaning, look it up in the dictionary! The context is often a clue to the meaning intended.

Double negatives

Try to phrase your message in a positive way rather than a negative one. Instead of:

a decision should not be delayed

write

a decision should be made

Always try and avoid multiple negatives, such as:

there is no reason to doubt that it is not true

The chances of the reader understanding that sentence as *true* or *not true* are about even!

Sometimes we can use a multiple negative to give an extra shade of meaning. For example:

> *There is no specific reason to doubt their claim, but previous experience . . .*

Before allowing this sort of negative construction to stand, make sure that it is really needed, either to make your point or add emphasis.

There are plenty of traps that the unwary writer can fall into. Those mentioned in this chapter are some of the most common. But don't let these pitfalls stop you writing. Just get it down on paper. The later process of editing should correct errors and idiocies.

CHAPTER 5

Sentences, paragraphs, punctuation and construction

'Learn to write well, or not to write at all.'

Dryden

5.1 Sentences

Ideally a sentence should deal with only one idea, and never more than two.

5.1.1 Definition

A common definition of a sentence is:

A group of words made up of one or more clauses; a clause is defined as having at least a subject and a verb.

Sentences may be *simple, compound* or *complex*. Sentences have a *subject* (who or what does the action), a *verb* (the action) and an *object* (to whom or what the action is done). There are also *clauses* (a short sentence, with a verb, within the sentence), and *phrases* (a group of linked words, without a verb, inside a sentence).

5.1.2 The parts of a sentence

Here is an easy compound sentence:

The manager	*SUBJECT* Who or what does the action. Who is spoken about.
who arrived from the northern office this morning	*CLAUSE* A short sentence within a sentence (it has a verb in it).
left	*VERB* The action.
headquarters	*OBJECT* To whom or what the action is done.
in the afternoon	*PHRASE* A group of linked words, without a verb, in a sentence.
and did not come back.	*FINAL CLAUSE*

5.1.3 Simple sentence

This is a complete statement at a basic level. It must have a subject and a verb. It usually has an object as well. For example:

I rode along.

The road was wet.

The car in front stopped.

The scooter braked.

The scooter hit the car.

I was injured.

These sentences are easy to understand but become boring if used too much. They are useful for presenting complicated information in a sequence, such as the example above.

5.1.4 Compound sentence

This has more than one subject and, often, more than one verb and object. For example:

The car and the scooter were driving along the road but then the car stopped at a zebra crossing.

5.1.5 Complex sentence

This has more than one clause and is really one sentence formed out of other, smaller sentences. For example:

> *The road was wet as I rode along and, although I braked when the car in front stopped at a zebra crossing, the scooter skidded and hit the car.*

Such sentences have variety, and more rhythm than the jerkiness of a series of simple sentences. But be careful not to make them too long and too complex.

Here is an example of a sentence built up from the simple to the very complex:

> *Productivity has fallen.*

Then, in a compound sentence, there are extra comments about the same subject, linked to the simple sentence by conjunctions such as 'and' and 'but', for example:

> *Productivity has fallen and is now lower than at any time in the last five years.*

In a complex sentence, the subject or object or both are qualified, for example:

Productivity, which is the principal factor in determining the level of profit, has fallen and is now lower than at any time in the last five years.

This is just about OK with a Clarity Index of about 37. It gets worse:

Productivity, which is the principal factor in determining the level of profit, has fallen and is now lower, as measured by input-output data for labour and for material, than at any time in the last five years.

But the ultimate complexity of such sentences comes by introducing yet another idea:

Productivity, which is the principal factor in determining the level of profit, has fallen and is now lower, as measured by input-output data for labour and for material, than at any time in the last five years, and moreover morale, which is at once influenced by the level of profit and by the standard of productivity is also correspondingly lower, though the principal reason for this cannot be determined with any degree of certainty.

It is impossible to read this sentence without a good deal of struggle to get some overall meaning. Such sentences are self-defeating – they confuse and obscure. And they are generally just pompous and showing off.

If you tend to compose long and involved sentences, then discipline yourself into using only simple and compound sentences. Any complex sentences should be revised into two or more simple ones. This also helps improve the logic of the writing, as simple sentences of single ideas can be sorted more easily into a readable sequence.

No one type of sentence is better than another, although some are more appropriate for particular purposes. Use a variety of types and vary the length of sentences. That way, your writing will be clearer and more readable.

5.2 Three *wrong* rules about sentences

There are three pieces of harmful advice about writing that many people learned at school. These so-called 'rules of grammar' are not rules, and never have been.

Do not begin sentences with 'and' or 'but'

Of course you may! 'And' and 'but' are conjunctions – they connect ideas. There are many useful conjunctions; good writers use them to flow smoothly from sentence to sentence. Otherwise short sentences would sound choppy. 'And' and 'but' are the most valuable of these connectors.

We all read sentences beginning with 'and' and 'but' every day. Most people never notice them. And that, incidentally, should reassure you that, if you do it intelligently, your reader will not notice them either. Do not go out of your way to begin sentences with 'and' or 'but', but do not avoid doing so when it seems natural.

Do not end sentences with prepositions

This has never been a rule of grammar or composition. Sometimes it is useful to end with a preposition; the alternative may be an awkward, unnatural sentence. A well known illustration of this is Winston Churchill's comment when criticised for ending a sentence with a preposition. Churchill shot back: 'This is the type of arrant pedantry up with which I will not put.'

However, prepositions are weak words; when a sentence ends with one it tends to fade out rather than end with authority. However, that may be better than going a long or awkward way around.

Do not repeat words

This is probably the worst advice of all. It often deprives you of the best words in key situations. Effective writing needs repetition of key words. Synonyms are often second-choice words, and there are very few exact synonyms. You are often forced from the specific to the abstract when you move from first-choice to second-choice words, for example:

Specific	Abstract
warehouse	facility
contract	document

Even if you do find an exact synonym, there is a risk of confusing the reader by using two (or more) words that stand for the same thing. To avoid over-repetition of nouns, use pronouns.

These three non-rules never have been rules of grammar. If it seems natural to begin a sentence with a conjunction, or end with a preposition, or repeat a good word, by all means do so. Your writing will read so naturally that readers will not notice you have done some things which they may have learned are wrong. Be natural. But grammar is important: do not go out of your way to throw out these 'rules' completely – they still have their uses.

5.3 Paragraphs

5.3.1 Basic guidelines

There is no absolute rule on paragraphing, but a guideline for starting a new paragraph is:

New topic   –   New paragraph

Contrast this with the idea of:

New thought   –   New sentence
(on same topic)

5.3.2 Paragraph length

The average length of paragraphs in any writing should not be more than about 15 lines. Paragraphs longer than this deter the reader and hamper communication. If you can deal with your topic in three lines, then have a three-line paragraph. But too many short paragraphs give a scrappy appearance, break the continuity of thought and can be 'jerky' and irritating to read. Some topics may need 20 or more lines of type which makes a daunting mass of text. Try to break it up and express the point more concisely.

5.3.3 The first sentence

A good technique is to use the first sentence to introduce a new topic and put your message strongly. The rest then elaborates or develops the point, or perhaps gives an example.

This technique also helps get the points across to the reader who scans through a report to get the gist. They often read only the first part of each paragraph. If you write to be scan read, you will be writing effectively.

5.4 Punctuation

5.4.1 Purpose

Written words represent the sounds of speech. In speech meaning is also conveyed by pausing and changing the tone of voice. In writing, punctuation marks perform this function. They tell the reader when a sentence is finished, when to pause in the middle, or how to interpret the words of the sentence. For example:

Woman without her man is a savage beast.

does not mean the same as:

Woman; without her, man is a savage beast.

or:

Woman, without her man, is a savage beast.

5.4.2 Punctuation and pauses

As a guide to punctuation, think of the main punctuation marks as representing pauses of different lengths:

Punctuation mark	Pause value
,	1
; :	2
. ? !	3

This simple guide will keep you out of punctuation trouble in most cases. Read aloud back through a passage you have written, pausing for a count of 1 at a comma, 2 at a semicolon, and so on. If you sound as though you have hiccups you probably have too many punctuation marks; if you run out of breath, you do not have enough.

5.5 Construction

5.5.1 Construction devices

It is important to present ideas in an attractive and interesting way that will catch the reader's attention. This is particularly so in long narrative writing. Here are some techniques that can be used:

• Make the main idea prominent, for example:

> *This unrest is not about wages or about the hours of work.* **It is about conditions.** *Conditions of service are important because they provide wages.*

The main idea is emphasised in the second sentence of four words.

• Use questions and answers, for example:

> *How can wages be higher, without an increase in unit cost?*

• Use constructions such as 'not this . . . but that' (though not necessarily using the same words), for example:

> *The reason for the high selling costs is not that the salesmen are poorly trained; most of them have been well trained for the type of customer they see. The reason is*

twofold. First, some of their calls are non-productive . . .
Secondly, much of their time is spent filling forms.

Other useful constructions are based on:

if . . . then

either . . . or

whether . . . or not

5.5.2 Variety

A piece of writing is often dull because it is monotonous in structure and in language. Variety is essential for interest. Among the ways of achieving variety are:

- varying the length of sentences;

- using comparisons, e.g. 'Alpha is cheaper; Beta is more expensive but lasts longer';

- varying the tenses;

- using imperatives occasionally;

- varying the length of paragraphs.

5.6 Summary

Keep to the guidelines on sentences – not more than 20 words. Vary the length with some shorter ones but do not make it too jumpy though. And keep to one idea, one sentence. Also paragraphs – not too long: 20 lines maximum, say 200 to 250 words. Keep to one theme per paragraph. Punctuate properly. Try speaking what you have written. Avoid monotony. Vary the writing with interesting constructions.

CHAPTER 6

Words, words, words

It is only in good writing that you will find how words are best used, what shades of meaning they can be made to carry, and by what devices (or lack of them) the reader is kept going smoothly or bogged down.

Jacques Barzun

6.1 So many words

Words are the 'building blocks' with which we speak and write in any language. English is particularly rich. There are about half a million entries in the *Shorter Oxford English Dictionary*.

But how many words do people actually need to know and use? The average, reasonably educated person may have a vocabulary of about three to four thousand words, but will use much less – perhaps between seven hundred and a thousand different words on an everyday basis. A very well-educated person, or a specialist in language, a journalist or a crossword freak for instance, might have a wider vocabulary – perhaps six to seven thousand – but they would not use even half of them in everyday speaking and writing.

6.2 Types of word

Words are classified into various categories according to the way they are used. This classification is knows as the 'parts of speech' – very useful for grammarians and academics to argue over! For a writer, however, it is sufficient to be able to distinguish what they all do, so as to use them correctly (which you will do, almost by instinct). This section gives a broad outline, sufficient for the present purpose.

6.2.1 Parts of speech

Nouns

These are naming words, of people, places and things. Examples are:

> *computer; factory; staff; country; France.*

The last example is a *proper noun*, because it names a particular example, a country.

The other examples are *common nouns*, because they identify a class of objects, people or places.

There are also *collective nouns*; examples are:

family; group; majority; percent, etc.

These indicate that numbers are involved.

Pronouns

These take the place of a noun, to avoid repeating the noun itself. Examples are:

he; her; it; them; who; that; which.

The last two examples are not always pronouns. *That* can also be:

- an adjective   –   'that machine';

- an adverb   –   'having gone that far';

- a conjunction   –   'the result was that people left early'.

Which can also be used as an adjective:

Which option do you prefer?

Adjectives

These are used to describe a noun, or another adjective. Examples are:

old; large; pale; strong; simple.

Verbs

These are 'doing' words, and can take many forms (tenses):

leave; arrived; will be; write; travelled; has been.

Adverbs

These modify a verb, an adjective or another adverb. Examples are:

quickly; suddenly; fairly; probably.

Many adverbs end in '-ly', and most words ending in '-ly' are adverbs.

Conjunctions or connectives

These are used to link words and phrases. Examples are:

and; or; but; that.

Remember, *that* is not always a conjunction; it can be used as a pronoun.

Prepositions

These show the relationship between words; usually between a noun (or pronoun) and another word or phrase. Examples are:

> came *after* dinner
>
> left *from* the back door
>
> a crate *of* empty bottles
>
> loaded *in* the machine
>
> checked the goods *for* quality

Interjections

These show surprise or emotion – an exclamation, usually at the start of a sentence. They have no grammatical function – use them very rarely or not at all in business writing. Examples are:

> *Oh! ah! Alas!*

(You may find the grammatical glossary in Appendix 6 helpful and interesting.)

6.2.2 Using personal pronouns in business writing

Traditionally, business writing has been in the formal style. There are two main reasons:

The document often goes to several people, so it is hard to write as if it were to a particular individual. The personal touch is lost.

Business writing, especially reports, should be factual and objective. Therefore objective-sounding language is used. Being objective drops directly into the passive voice:

> *The site of the accident was visited.*
> *It is considered that . . .*
> *It has been shown that . . .*

We are expressing personal opinions – the thus passive voice is often used to give pseudo-objectivity to those opinions. The usual result is long, clumsy sentences.

Nowadays, you can use the first person in reports, so write in the active voice. You will get simpler, clearer sentences:

> *I visited the site of the accident.*
> *I think . . .*
> *We found that . . .*

You can also mix 'I' and 'we' in the same text. Use 'I' for the things you did personally; use 'we' where you are stating, for example, your department's or organisation's conclusions. But be consistent in your use of 'I' and 'we'. Using the first person sounds natural when expressing opinions, such as in the conclusions section.

When describing methods or results, keep the factual information sounding objective – use the third person. Wherever possible, however, make the verb active, by starting the sentence with the main subject.

6.3 Four practical rules

6.3.1 Prefer the familiar to the unfamiliar word

Good writing is built up from familiar words; the effective writer will stick to them, for example:

> 'Indicate the route to my abode'

is a ridiculous way of saying

> 'Show me the way to go home'

Good style in writing and speaking will be made more interesting by the very occasional use of less familiar words. But do this only when the occasion is right – only when the unfamiliar word counts fully. This is as true of good rhetoric (speechmaking) as it is of good writing.

For example, Abraham Lincoln's Gettysburg address would lose impact if it opened:

> 'Eighty-seven years ago . . .'

instead of

'Fourscore and seven years ago . . .'

But this is rhetoric – appropriate in speech but not really suitable in writing. So, prefer the short, everyday word to the longer, less familiar one. Do not overuse words like:

requirements	(needs)
utilise	(use)
commence	(start)
proceed	(go)
termination	(end)

Longer words cause little problem on their own. But, when there are several of them together in one sentence, it becomes heavy and difficult to read quickly. For example:

I have endeavoured to ascertain
(I have tried to find out)

Numbers have assumed such proportions that . . .
(There are now so many that . . .)

Choose words that the readers will understand easily. It is not professional or clever to use unusual words, just inconsiderate.

Also, avoid non-English words and phrases. The very occasional use of them may add to your style – but only if it is the *mot juste* (see Appendix 5).

6.3.2 Prefer the concrete word to the abstract

'The higher the degree of abstraction the greater the difficulty of communication' is a fundamental truth. To be sure of communication, use precise concrete terms which stand for things the reader can picture, for example:

> *Increasing the call frequency should lead to improvements in the account retention index.*

Just about understandable, but horribly pretentious! The sentence is more meaningful as:

> *Calling on customers more often will stop them changing to other suppliers.*

or:

> *Unsuitable conditions caused further labour turnover.*

means less than

> *Mrs Lee left because she could not stand the smell from the kitchen.*

Search your work for abstractions. Try to avoid them, or at least ensure that the meaning is clear. Typical examples are:

Situation	*Facilities*
Conditions	*Significant*

Relations	*Improvements*
Principles	*Development*
Relative	*Comparative*

6.3.3 Prefer one word to many

Brevity improves both the readability and the effectiveness of any writing. Edit ruthlessly – cut out one-third or more of the words. It will then be a much better document. An example from real life is as follows:

> *It will, of course, be appreciated that the cost of such a survey must be directly related to the calibre of the staff assigned to the project, and the depth to which the study is taken.*

This is tortuous, understandable only with difficulty and has a Clarity Index of about 44.

Instead, this passage could have read:

> *The cost will depend on the level of the staff used and on the depth of the survey.*

If it had, it would have been straightforward and easy to understand.

6.3.4 Prefer the short word to the long, and the Anglo-Saxon to the Latin (and use the correct word)

Here are some examples of longer, mainly Latin, words with their shorter, mainly Anglo-Saxon, equivalents:

accomplish	–	do
ascertain	–	find out
characterise	–	describe
demonstrate	–	show
elucidate	–	make clear
exterior	–	outside
fabricate	–	build
facilitate	–	make easy
inaccurate	–	wrong
individuals	–	people
manufacture	–	make
obligation	–	duty
participate	–	take part
probability	–	chance
remunerate	–	pay
rigorous	–	strict
subsequently	–	later
terminate	–	end
ulterior	–	hidden
utilisation	–	use

The longer, left-hand column words are often abstractions, which also adds to the difficulty in understanding them. Avoid this type of word whenever possible. However, they may have specific meanings or usages, so their use is not altogether forbidden. So, if it is absolutely necessary to use a long rare word, make sure it is used correctly. And make sure you correctly understand the word you are using.

It is easy to confuse one word with a similar word:

propound	and	*expound*
uninterested	and	*disinterested*
discreet	and	*discrete*

These are typical examples of such confusions, which are often known as *malapropisms* (from a character in an eighteenth-century play, who frequently misused words).

Language is constantly changing: many hundreds of new words come into the language each year; others acquire new meanings, and some go out of use. The real danger is when we do not realise that a word now has another or additional meaning, or when a word is in the process of changing its meaning, but does not yet have an agreed definition.

Finally, remember that other people's vocabulary is probably different to yours. We all know some unusual words – but they are not always the same ones!

6.4 Spelling

There is only one certain rule to follow when in doubt about the spelling of any word in the English language: look it up in a dictionary. If you cannot find the word in a normal dictionary – because you do not know how to spell it! – use a specialist spelling dictionary, which lists words in the ways they are commonly misspelled, as well as in the correct way.

Spelling is important. If you do not spell correctly, you have two potential problems:

- people may misunderstand you (for example if you confuse *principle* and *principal*);

- your reader may consider you illiterate or careless – or both.

As a result, your message will lose credibility (see Appendix 3).

6.5 The active and passive voices in verbs

There are two different ways of using verbs to express action. Active verbs are the best words for showing action. Passive verbs are dull, lack force and make poor reading. The use of an active verb helps to gain the reader's attention.

In the active voice the main subject of the sentence does something:

The cat sat on the mat.

You hit him.

The new computer system has reduced the time needed to process an order.

In the passive voice the main subject of the sentence has something done to it:

The mat was sat upon by the cat.

He was hit by you.

The time needed to process an order has been reduced with the new computer system.

Prefer the active voice

Your writing will be simpler and more forceful if you use active rather than passive verbs. The passive voice will usually lead to longer and more complex sentences, which is clumsy and boring.

But the passive voice is necessary in our writing, and there are occasions when the passive is correct. Also we may wish to record that a thing was done, rather than who did it. But overuse gives the feeling of hesitancy and weakens the impact of the writing. Do not hide behind the passive to avoid responsibility.

Consider this example:

Passive: *In designing the sampling scheme, it was found that a problem was created by the seasonal nature of*

demand which could only be overcome by rescheduling the
investigation.

Active: *The seasonal pattern of demand created a problem*
for the design of the sampling scheme. Rescheduling the
investigation was the only way of overcoming this.

It is obvious which passage is easier to read and understand. The passive has a far higher clarity index than the active, mainly because of its tortured construction. So the active version is much easier to understand; also the passive sentence contains three passive verbs. This can also create ambiguities; the sentence may be interpreted in more than one way. Use of the active voice will avoid a lot of uncertainty.

6.6 Jargon

Jargon is a precise technical language which cannot be understood without training or experience in the relevant subject. It has the effect of dividing people into insiders and outsiders. If the reader is an outsider, he will feel resentful, and the document may fail to communicate.

Computer nerds are prime culprits in assuming other (innocent) people know what they are writing about. In reality only other computer nerds will understand.

Therefore, use specialist jargon only when it is essential shorthand that you know your reader will understand. Otherwise explain your technical terms; include a glossary as an appendix. And be very careful about using everyday words in a specialist sense. Jargon has a precise technical meaning and there are situations when it is needed. Good rules to follow are:

- Ask and answer the question: 'What do my readers know about this subject – and its jargon?

- Use as little jargon as possible.

- If it is the best word for the job, then use it.

- If in any doubt – define it.

Generally it is safe to use the reader's business jargon, provided you observe these points. But never use the 'gibberish' jargon that is really just a long-winded way of saying something the *Oxford Dictionary* describes as 'barbarous and debased language'.

6.7 Clichés

A cliché is a worn out group of words which has been over-used. It adds nothing to a sentence, usually reduces its impact, and is often meaningless. Such expressions are often scribbled down without thought if we are writing fast. They are a convenient sort of shorthand which saves us trying to think of a better phrase at the time. Avoid them and cut them out when revising.

Some examples are as follows:

It should be noted that . . .

It will be appreciated that . . .

Very careful consideration . . .

From this point of view . . .

In relation to . . .

Explore avenues . . .

In the case of . . .

In the event that . . .

At this moment in time . . .

You will have many more of this sort of cliché. Scour them from your writing – it will read much better.

6.7.1 Cliché definitions in reports

The following phrases frequently occur in business writing, especially reports. Beside each one is suggested what they probably mean. Avoid the trap of using phrases such as these.

Phrase:	Probable true meaning:
It has long been known . . .	I haven't bothered to look up the original reference.
Of great theoretical and practical importance . . .	Interesting to me.

While it has not been possible to provide definite answers to these questions . . .	My theories didn't work out.
Three of the examples were chosen for detailed study.	The results of the others didn't make sense and were ignored.
Typical results are shown.	The best results are shown.
These results will be reported at a later date.	I might get around to this sometime.
It is believed that . . .	I think . . .
It is generally believed that . . .	A couple of other people think so too.
It might be argued that . . .	I shall now raise this objection because I have such a good answer for it.
It is clear that much additional work will be required before a complete understanding . . .	I don't understand it.
This was simply a question of market forces.	I haven't a clue why this happened.

It is a staggering fact that . . .	I've only just realised . . .
Having said that . . .	This could go either way, so I'm going to cover myself.
What I don't understand is . . .	What I understand but don't agree with is . . .
A great deal of thought has been given to . . .	I haven't thought about it.

Using this sort of fraudulent expression will quickly indicate to the reader that you have taken little trouble over the document. Also you probably know less about the subject of the report than they do. This kind of sloppiness is deceitful and dangerous; remember people are taking decisions on the basis of what you write.

CHAPTER 7

Editing, layout, numbers and graphics

'Every author's Fairy Godmother should provide, not only a pen but also a blue pencil.'

F. L. Lucas, *Style*

7.1 Starting to edit

When you have finished your writing, read the typed draft through completely from start to finish. Do this before starting to work on it in detail; it is the only way to get any feel of its overall impact; the way it will strike the reader. While reading, mark passages which need attention. Do not stop to deal with them, but answer these questions in your mind and make notes:

• Does it *look* good?

• Is it 'readable' – language, style, vocabulary?

- Is the material presented in the most logical and orderly sequence?

- Are the arguments easy to follow?

- Do they build persuasively to your conclusions and recommendations?

- Is it a convincing document?

Having raised all these questions, go back to the passages you have marked for detailed attention.

7.1.1 Minor editing

When you read over a piece that you have written, you may realise it does not say exactly what you mean. If you have to reread it to understand it, you know it is not clear enough. We need to do some minor editing to make the message clear. Often a change of wording here, some revised punctuation there, is enough. Sometimes though, this is not enough.

7.1.2 Major rewrite

If the problem is more serious, say the way in which we have organised our thoughts or constructed our sentences, then minor editing is not usually enough. It is better to start again from scratch.

- Take the unsatisfactory paragraphs, and pick out and note down the key points you are trying to make.

- Put the original version, with which you are not happy, out of sight. This is important. If you keep the original in sight you will inevitably refer back to it. The danger is that you will again use the wording and construction that has caused the need for revision.

- Then, from your rough notes, structure the points into a logical sequence.

- Now rewrite the paragraph(s) using the revised structure and notes. Revise until you are sure that what is written is exactly what you mean and is clear and concise.

- Finally, check that the new paragraph(s) fit into the flow of the original, in place of the paragraph(s) they replace. If not, edit them so they *do* fit.

7.1.3 Revision

Now return to the beginning of the text and start the painstaking work of detailed revision. This is done by using a systematic 'checklist' of questions.

Interval for reflection

But first, try to leave your work at least overnight, and preferably several days, before starting revision. The reason for this is that, even with the editing you have already done, it is likely to be:

- *Poorly arranged.* Some sections may be better suited to another part of the argument.

- *Illogical.* Some of the conclusions may be invalid, or they may be valid but not proven by the facts given.

- *Poorly expressed.* Is it written throughout in clear, lucid and expressive words? Unlikely.

- *Unreadable.* The sentences may be too long, the paragraph divisions poorly chosen, and so on.

All is not lost – these faults can be put right by revision, a difficult but satisfying activity.

7.2 Editing

The following checklist is arranged, section by section, in the order in which the sections should appear in a report. For documents other than reports the checklist is still valid. Use the relevant sections.

The checklist method may seem laborious, but as you become more accustomed to revising your work in this way, many of the more obvious questions will become redundant and your progress through the report will be quicker. This approach ensures that no important aspect is ignored during revision.

Title page

- Is the title concise but detailed enough to indicate the scope of the report?

- Do the 'key words' of the subject stand out for immediate identification and future reference?

- Author/s?

- Recipient/s and their titles and/or departments where relevant?

- Date?

- Reference/file number?

Contents

- Is the list of contents complete?

- Is it sufficiently detailed (or over-detailed)?

- Does the position of each section match the page references?

- Is a list of illustrations and visual material included?

- Are all appendices listed in order and with page references?

Summary

- Is it the *briefest* possible statement of the whole report?

- Is it an *accurate* representation of the whole report?

- Is it *complete* and *independent* – can it stand on its own without further reference to the full report?

Introduction

- Are the terms of reference stated fully – in the introduction or elsewhere in the report?

- Authorising person/body?

- Investigating person/body, i.e. author's name?

- Method of enquiry; scope and coverage of the investigation?

- Is the background as brief as possible? Is there enough general data to enable understanding?

- Does it *exclude* all specific data belonging properly to the main text?

Findings

- *Flow.* Text follows naturally from the introduction?

- *Order.* Logical? Due prominence to main factors? Beginning and end 'focus points'? Priorities right?

- *Clarity.* Language clear and precise?

- *Brevity.* Statements as succinct as possible?

- *Accuracy.* All the facts and figures correct?

- *Quantity.* Sufficient data to support arguments? Too much data? Is all inessential data excluded? Any important section lacking? Anything overlooked?

- *Balance.* Do the different sections have a fair proportion of the space available? Are minor topics adequately discussed?

- *Adverse factors.* Are they dealt with fairly?

- *Purpose.* Does the purpose of the report come across clearly?

- *Persuasion.* Is the tone fair-minded? Do arguments lead inevitably to your conclusions?

Conclusions

- Do these flow naturally from the text?

- Every conclusion fully supported?

- Any unsupported "opinions" or decisions?

- Conclusions reflect sound analysis of the information?

- Is analysis based on:

- – wide experience?

- – comparison with a similar situation?

- – intuitive feel?

- Alternative conclusions discussed?

Recommendations

- Each listed *separately,* corresponding to conclusions?

- Clear what *action* is required?

- *Practical* not theoretical?

- *Relevant* to the terms of reference?

- Do they solve the problem?

- *Appropriate* to the situation?

- Stand out clearly as 'action centre' of the report?

Layout

- Appearance encourage reading?

- Good balance – space to print?

- Headings and numbering adequate?

- Layout highlight most important features?

Appendices

- All there?

- Numbered?

- In the order related to the text?

- All necessary?

- Any better placed in the text?

- Glossary?

- List of abbreviations?

Acknowledgements/References/Bibliography

- Complete?

- Visuals?

- All there?

- Properly positioned in the text?

- Accurately produced?

- Any more that would be useful?

At the end of the revision process, you should have an inviting document about half to two-thirds the length of the original. What you have shed in weight you will have increased in clarity. The reader-appeal of a pithy, clear, complete and correct report is enormous. The lean look will do half your job of persuasion for you.

7.3 Reviewing a report

It is hard to be objective when you review your own work. We have tight deadlines and, having completed writing a report, the last thing we want to do is rewrite it!

However, it is essential that the report achieves its objective. If it does not, we have wasted time writing it and researching the subject of the report.

7.3.1 Reviewing hints

When you have the final draft, put it aside for two or three days and then read it again. With luck, you will see it from the reader's point of view rather than your own.

Ask an experienced person to review the document and make their comments, using the checklist below of key reviewing points.

Use the model reviewing checklist yourself to question the purpose, structure, clarity of writing and finished appearance.

Finally, ask again the key question:

Will the report will achieve its purpose?

7.3.2 Checklist for reviewing

Objective achieved?

• Do I, as the reader, know what I am now expected to do?

• Would I be likely to do what the writer requests/expects?

Reader(s) considered?

• Their knowledge considered?

• Their interests met?

Structure and content sound?

• Logical sequence?

• Conclusions justified by facts?

• Opinions and facts distinguished?

• Any inaccuracies noted?

• Any unnecessary material included?

Written clearly and concisely?

• Unusual words?

• 'Waffley' phrases?

- Jargon?

- Long sentences?

- Vague statements/abstractions?

- Ambiguities?

- Complex sentences?

- Active or passive?

- Helpful punctuation?

- Good use of paragraphs?

- The right style – formal/friendly?

Attractively presented?

- Good margins and spacing?

- Helpful headings?

- Effective use of tables/diagrams?

7.4 Making a summary

7.4.1 What is a summary?

Whatever it is called – abstract, digest, précis, summary, executive summary – it is always the same thing: the briefest possible statement of the subject matter of a longer document. The summary will be the last section written. It must remain faithful to the original, it must cover *all* the essential points and it must be fully understandable by itself. It is *not* a list of extracts, highlights or notes on the original. It will appear early on in the report as an 'overview' for the readers. It may also be the *only* section read by some readers.

The purpose of a summary

The précis may have all or any of these functions:

- an introduction to the subject;

- a guide to readers as to whether the document is of any interest to them;

- a time-saver for busy executives – preliminary decisions are often based on a reading of the summary and the recommendations;

- for yourself, a check that you have actually said what you intended to say.

7.4.2 Guidelines

- Ensure that you are clear about the purpose of the summary and who the readers are:

- What do you want them to get from the summary?

- Which part of your report do you expect them to turn to after reading the summary?

- The summary must be self-contained. The reader should be able to get a clear view without going into any other part of the text – except for supporting detail. For a lengthy document it is useful to include page references in brackets, referring to the section being summarised. This will help the reader(s) to take a quick glance at areas of particular interest to them.

- Make sure it answers the questions:

  - Why is the report being produced?

  - How have we gone about the task which is the subject of the report?

  - What are the key findings?

  - What do those findings mean?

  - What should we do now?

- Do not include anything in the summary that is not already in the text.

- Write it in conversational English. Do not use jargon – the summary may be read by people who have no relevant technical background. Do not write the summary in condensed English – 'telegraphese'. It may be useful, however, to have bullet point lists of key points.

- Keep it short. Aim for a length of not more than 5 per cent of the main body of the text. So, for a 20-page report, not more than 1 page. However, if the report is a long one, say over 50 pages, keep the summary to 2–3 per cent; for a 100-page report 2–3 pages at most.

7.4.3 The process

The key steps in the summarising process refer equally to a writer's own work, or a summary of someone else's work:

- Read the whole document.

- Identify and summarise the central theme.

- Study section by section. Identify and summarise the main statement of each section.

- As you read, cut out: repetition, lists, examples, detailed description. Replace these by short general statements.

- Combine into a continuous narrative. Be brief without losing sense or clarity of expression. Give an overview, not the detail.

- Read through the summary. Ask:

- does it give a correct impression of the original?

- will it make sense to the reader separate from the full report?

7.5 Layout

How the document is presented will affect the way in which it is received. It is not necessary to be a graphics designer in order to achieve impact in presentation. Follow the layout and ideas in this chapter to get good-looking reports which demand to be read.

7.5.1 Writing

The finished layout will be influenced by the way you write. But there are three things you can do that will give a more attractive layout and will help the reader:

- Keep paragraphs short.

- Use headings, as signposts for the readers.

- Use lists.

As well as helping the reader understand your writing, these points will create more 'white space' on the page. This makes the document look more attractive than a page of close type.

7.5.2 Spacing

Margins

Leave plenty of margin all round the page. The exact size is a matter of choice or house style. A reasonable suggestion is:

- Left-hand margin 30 mm. This ensures that words will not be hidden when the page is filed or bound.

- Right-hand margin 20 mm. This stops the page looking too crowded.

- Top and bottom margins at least 20 mm.

This space will give a pleasing open feel to the page.

Paragraph indentation

Indent subparagraphs to the right. This is the best way of showing its subordination. The space helps the reader to see the structure, and adds visual appeal.

Indenting the first line of a new paragraph is a matter of personal taste. It is more often found in books than in business writing. Also, leave space between paragraphs – one and a half or two lines is sufficient.

7.5.3 Numbering

Sections

The decimal system is widely known and infinitely flexible, but do not let it run to more than three figures, for example:

1	main headings
1.1	subheadings
1.1.1	sub-subheadings

An alternative is to mix different types of letters and numbers, for example:

I	capital Roman numbers – main report sections
A	capital letters – headings
1	ordinary numbers – subheadings
a	small letters – sub-subheadings
i	small Roman numbers – individual points

But be consistent in whatever system you use.

With any system, do not over-number; it is not necessary. You can identify items in a list with 'bullet points':

- dots

* asterisks

or any other symbol available on your printer.

The numbering method used in this book is decimal. It is clear and simple.

Pages

Number all pages. Place page numbers in an outer right-hand corner where they can be easily seen when reading through the text.

7.5.4 Typography

Typefaces

Use different typefaces within the text for emphasis, and for indicating different levels of heading. Do not overdo it – keep to one main typeface and use **bold** or *italic* for emphasis as we have in this book.

Modern word processing systems can improve presentation greatly; they can also ruin the presentation when over-elaborate.

Levels and type style for headings

Distinguish:

Main headings

Subheadings

Sub-subheadings

It is best to do this with different type styles as we have in this book.

Spacing

Leave more space before a main heading than before a subheading, and so on. Also, make sure that a heading is close to the paragraph to which it relates. Do not allow headings to float between paragraphs.

Page headers or footers

It will help readers to know where they are if the heading, and any section number, is repeated at the top or foot of each page. It is a valuable aid to continuity in a report.

7.5.5 Materials

Paper

In general, use good quality standard A4 size white paper; however, for special sections you might find it useful to include coloured paper. This helps the reader to quickly pick out sections, such as appendices.

You can use larger pages for appendices if you want readers to refer to a diagram or table while they are reading Copy the diagram onto the right-hand half of an A3 page, so that it can be folded out for reference.

Dividers

Use lightweight card or slightly heavier quality paper (say 120 gsm) to create dividers. These will enable the reader to go straight to a particular section. The dividers can be coloured, or they could be tabbed – both methods make for ease of reference.

Binding

Any substantial document will look more professional in a binder. There are many binding systems on the market; whatever binding system you use, make it appropriate for the amount of handling the document will receive. If it will get a lot of use and many people will read it, then the binding needs to be robust. If it is a one-off affair that will simply get stacked, then bind accordingly.

7.5.6 House style

You may have a house style with rules to follow. These may affect the structure of a report as well as the layout. For example:

- Always start with a summary.

- Section headings must always be in capitals.

A house style saves you the trouble of structuring and laying out a report from scratch each time. It also helps readers find their way through a familiar format.

If you do not already have a house style, it may be a good idea to establish one that will meet your needs and those of your readers.

An attractive businesslike layout adds to the authority of what you have to say. It will also help your readers find their way to the particular information they want. There is considerable scope for good layout to attract the readers and help them understand the content.

7.6 Numbers and graphics

7.6.1 Numbers in writing

No one agrees about how numbers should be expressed in ordinary writing: in figures, or in words? There are four guidelines that should suit most readers.

- Write single numbers (one to nine) in words. Use figures for any number larger than nine.

- Do not start a sentence with a figure: spell it out; or avoid it.

- Use figures for things that are basically numerical, such as: age, money, percentage, weight, size, addresses.

- Do not mix figures and words in a list.

There may be special cases, for example if you are reproducing part of another document, or other evidence when the words and numbers are mixed. But, apart from these instances, if you keep to the guidelines above numerical reference will be clear.

7.6.2 Tables

Here are some guidelines for producing easy to understand tables.

* Give the table a heading, a title specific to that table. It should indicate the relationship you want to bring out, not just the general subject matter.

* Keep tables small. Divide large tables into separate ones unless it is essential that all the relationships be shown together.

* List figures that are to be compared vertically. It is easier to compare the numbers than when they are laid out horizontally.

* Only include the figures the readers need; show them in a way that makes them easy to understand and compare.

* Vertical columns form their own eye-guide and do not need rulings. Use vertical rules only for separating different types of information, e.g. row categories from data, data from totals.

* Horizontal rules help guide the eye. Break large blocks of data every 5th row, but with a double space rather than a rule.

- Try to make classifications specific and mutually exclusive. Avoid overlapping categories (such as 10–20, 20–30).

- Avoid open-ended classes ('500 and over'), especially if their contents are at all significant.

- Specify units of measurement clearly. Prefer words to powers of numbers, for example thousands or 000 rather than 1^3.

- Where columns are to be compared, put them next to each other.

- Put columns of percentages or averages next to the data to which they relate.

- Do not show derived figures (percentages, for example) to look more precise than warranted by the original data.

- Round off all figures to 3 or even 2 effective digits unless you are dealing with minute variations.

- Avoid lots of footnotes, but do include the source of any data that is not your own.

Examples of tables

Where the data is simple and there are only a few variables, an open unlined format as shown in Figure 7.1 can be used.

Manufacturing Sector				
	No. of companies	No. of employees	Salaries £m	Fixed assets end of year £m
Food	110	14,631	32.7	122.5
Beverages	6	1,078	35.7	150.5
Textiles	18	733	6.1	9.5
Wood and products	23	955	12.4	29.3
Paper and products	20	937	24.7	36.9
Chemicals and products	24	895	23.0	88.8
Non-metallic products	28	1,170	15.4	60.1
Machinery and equipment	41	1,609	46.0	106.6
Other	8	121	18.1	24.4

Figure 7.1 A simple four-column spread table.

Where there is a lot of information vertical lines help to distinguish sections. In the example shown in Figure 7.2, the text has been spread right across the page, so that the book will have to be turned sideways to read it. If space is not too much of a consideration, the information could be blocked out and the text filled into the A4 page vertically. This would make it both easier to read and easier to grasp the related information. With a lot of information, horizontal lining can be helpful. But the resulting grid pattern may not be pleasing to read, as the eye jumps from box to box.

Date	Event	Description	Venue	Country	Contact
06/10/2000 10/09/2000	Fair	Bife-Timb – Int'l specialised fair for furniture, wooden products, furniture fittings, interior decorations, machinery & equip. for forest exploitation and wood processing.	Bucharest	Romania	Romexpo – see below.
08/11/2000 10/11/2000	Exhibition	InterFood Poland and InterFoodTech	Warsaw	Poland	Alex Hogg, ITE – see below.
08/10/2000 12/10/2000	Mission	Trade Mission to Poland		Poland	Ken Aldred, Nottinghamshire County Council (tel 0115 977 2050).
09/10/2000 14/10/2000	Fair	TIB – Bucharest Trade Fair	Bucharest	Romania	The British Romanian Chamber of Commerce, PO Box 367, 509 Footscray Rd, London SE9 3UJ (tel 020 8302 0310; fax 020 8309 1321).
09/10/2000 14/10/2000	Exhibition	Re-Trade – Int'l exh. of second-hand machinery & equipment/Inventika – Int'l exh. of inventions, scientific research and new technologies	Bucharest	Romania	Romexpo – see below.
10/10/2000 13/10/2000	Exhibition	Construction, Houseware/Furniture and Interior	Donetsk	Ukraine	Victor Maximenko, Specialised Exhibition Centre, Cheliuskintsev, Str. 189-B, Donetsk, Ukraine 340048 (tel 00 0622 577830; 3812155; email expodon@dol.donetsk.ua).
11/10/2000 15/10/2000	Exhibition	International Furniture: interior decoration and supporting industry fair	Split	Croatia	Zagreb Fair – see below.
11/10/2000 15/10/2000	Fair	Automobile industry	Split	Croatia	Standform, Sine, Poljicka cesta bb, 21000 Split, Croatia (tel/fax: 00 383 (0) 21 324252).
12/10/2000 14/10/2000	Exhibition	Baltic Fish 20000	Kaliningrad	Russia	Mr Pjotr Gritsenko, Baltic Expo, Okjabrskaya ul, 3a, 2360060 Kaliningrad, Russia (tel: 0 7 0112 34109; fax: 0 7 0112 341095).
16/10/2000 20/10/2000	Mission	Trade Mission to Croatia	Zagreb	Croatia	Nicola Brown, Executive World Trade, London Chamber of Commerce & Industry, 33 Queen Street, London EC4R 1AP (tel: 0171 248 4444; fax: 0171 203 1905).

Source: EETC: Exhibitions and fairs.

Figure 7.2 Example of a table carrying complex information.

7.6.3 Using graphics and visual aids

Graphics are very useful; they save words, clarify information and help the reader understand the message quickly and clearly. We often understand by comparing and find it easier to see comparisons with graphical illustrations. There are many kinds of graphics, from photographs, to line drawings, to diagrams, to paintings, to charts. The three main types of chart are bar charts, pie charts and graphs. Each has its own benefits and drawbacks; we give guidelines on using them effectively.

Visuals aid understanding. They do not rely on words to communicate, but use an extra sense. They give a lot of information, quickly and clearly, and provide variety for the reader. Visual aids are easy to remember; they simplify and make the appearance of a document more attractive. But note the following:

- Visual material must be very well done – poor diagrams lose more than they gain.

- Put visual material in the main body, close to its relevant text.

- Try to place visual material the same way up as the text.

- Use colour photographs but make sure they are well produced. Use colour for diagrams, and ensure clear drawing and shading for best effect.

- If you use visual material for a report, find out how it is to be reproduced; make sure the diagrams etc. are ready on time.

7.6.4 Bar charts

These are the most widely used, and have the least danger of misleading the reader. It is easy to draw comparisons between the figures in Figure 7.3.

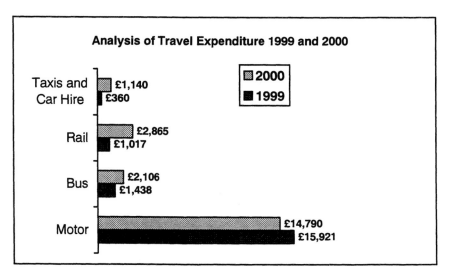

Figure 7.3 Example of a bar chart.

Bar charts are better than graphs for showing changes over time, as in the example above. They are also useful for showing sales of different products, variations by region, and so on, where these do not occur in any particular order. Graphs are less use in such cases.

Guidelines

•   Give the chart a specific title.

•   Make sure the bars start at zero, so that the lengths are proportional to the amounts.

•   Label all bars.

•   Give each bar a figure to show the amount.

•   Leave a space between bars. But if the bars are on a time scale, or represent a sequence of quantities, the bars should touch (see Figure 7.4).

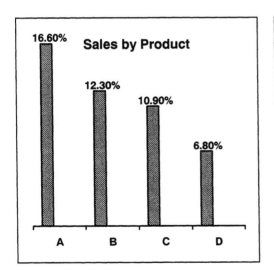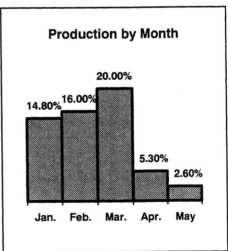

Figure 7.4 Spacing of bars in a bar chart.

It does not matter whether the bars are horizontal or vertical. Use whichever best fits the space available. However, a time scale always goes across, giving vertical bars.

7.6.5 Pie charts

These give a visual impression of how a total is made up. However, it is often difficult to compare segments within a pie chart; and even more difficult to compare the segments of one pie chart with those of another. In the example shown in Figure 7.5, the slight change in segment sizes is hardly noticeable. The figures could probably have been illustrated more effectively with a bar chart.

Motor Expenses

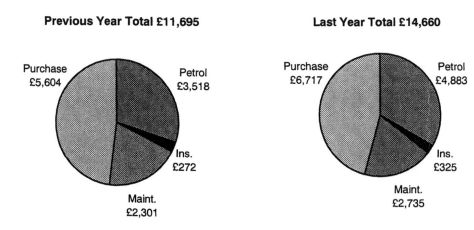

Previous Year Total £11,695

Purchase £5,604   Petrol £3,518   Ins. £272   Maint. £2,301

Last Year Total £14,660

Purchase £6,717   Petrol £4,883   Ins. £325   Maint. £2,735

Figure 7.5 Pie charts.

Guidelines

- Give the chart a title.

- Label each segment of the pie and give a quantity or percentage. Make sure the colour or shading of a segment does not obscure the label and figures.

- Do not make the chart over-complex by:

  – having too many segments – say, no more than five or six;

  – using shading that does not reproduce clearly.

What looks good on a computer screen may not come out so well when reduced in size and photocopied in black and white (or colour).

Three-dimensional pie charts can give undue emphasis to the segment nearest the reader (see Figure 7.6).

If you need different sized pies because the total amounts are different, do not exaggerate the difference – keep the areas in proportion.

7.6.6 Graphs

Graphs are invaluable, but reproduction is not easy. If the computer output is not clear draw the graph yourself.

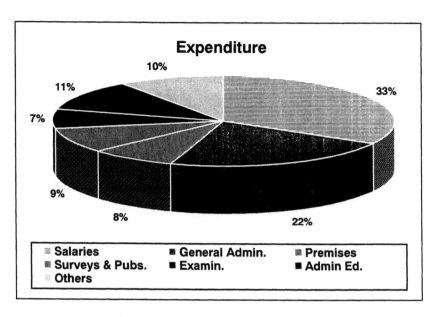

Figure 7.6 Three-dimensional pie chart.

A graph should not distort the facts. Zero must always be shown; where this is difficult, show zero with an interruption in the scales. The ratio of the horizontal to the vertical scale must be reasonable; a rough guide is that the centre of gravity of the curve should lie between 40 and 60 per cent of the vertical scale. The distance between its highest and lowest points should not exceed half the vertical scale.

Graphs are good for showing trends, fluctuations and the relationship between two variables. However, a graph makes a claim about every point along a line, so use it only if you are confident in making that claim. Also, by drawing a graph, you are usually claiming that a change in one variable is caused by changes in the other. Graphs with many variable lines become complex and not easy to understand.

Guidelines

- Select scales so you are filling them both; this normally gives lines going diagonally across the graph.

- The axes (scale lines) are generally drawn with the vertical scale to the left and the horizontal scale extending from it to the right. Where they meet is zero.

- Show zeros: don't mislead. Break the scale if necessary to show zero.

- The scale for the change observed goes up the side. The cause of the change goes across the bottom. Time scales always go across horizontally.

- Give clear dimensions for both scales.

- Give the graph a specific, informative title.

- Leave the original points when drawing a trend line.

- Do not draw a line through scattered points.

- Do not extend the line or fill in gaps without very good reason.

- Either put figures on the points or leave the grid in so that the values can be read off.

- Do not have more than three or four lines of comparison on a graph.

Figure 7.7 shows some examples of graphs.

7.6.7 Other types of illustration

Photographs, drawings and diagrams

As well as charts and graphs other types of illustration can be used:

- photographs can nowadays be photocopied very well onto plain paper, and in colour if required;

- line drawings;

- maps;

- line diagrams such as flowcharts, layouts, organisation charts, isometric drawings, etc.

Whatever method of reproduction is used for drawings and diagrams, there are three guidelines:

- The illustration should fill (but not overflow) the page. If there is text and an illustration on the page, balance and harmonise the space given to each.

- Use templates for drawing the various symbols.

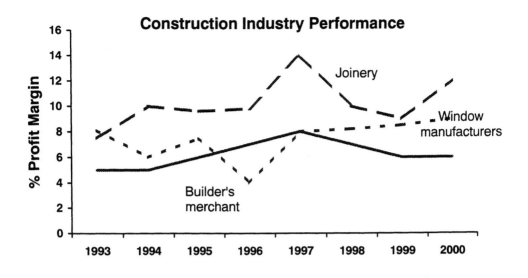

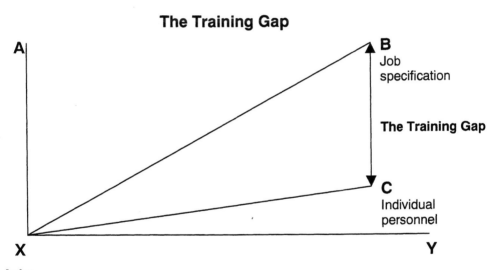

Axis:
XA Skills and knowledge item by item (it could be the more items the higher the grade or remuneration).
XB Skills and knowledge required in job specifications.
XC The individual's skills and knowledge.
XY Time line or time as at line with projected time plan.

Figure 7.7 Examples of graphs.

- Unless you are a competent letterer, use Lettraset or have the wording typed.

Pictograms

They are not as easy to produce as charts and nearly always mislead. Be wary of using them but, at a simple level, they can occasionally be useful.

As a general guideline, if you show pictures of different sizes (sacks, barrels, etc.) to represent different quantities, ensure that it is done without misleading.

7.6.8 Deciding on an illustration

The use of illustrations should be planned; illustrations should not added as an afterthought. Before deciding to use an illustration, ask what purpose it will serve:

- Will it save words?

- Will it really clarify things for the readers and help them understand?

- Will it help them make comparisons?

- To what specific points are we trying to draw their attention?

Then think about the production of the illustration:

- What resources are available?

- Will the cost of production be worthwhile?

- How will it be linked with the text? In the text? Alongside it? Right way up? In an appendix? Also you can have illustrations on larger pages that fold out.

Finally, do not make the illustrations too complex. Computer software packages produce fancy graphics which can be a menace! Keep it simple. If the readers have to struggle to understand the illustration, it has failed in its purpose.

CHAPTER 8

Memos, minutes, manuals

Sir Laurence: Send me a memo, Miss Jones.

Miss Jones: Yes, sir, what about?

Sir Laurence: I am to remember the 5th of November for some reason.

Miss Jones: Yes sir, it's your wife's birthday!

1930s farce

8.1 Memos

8.1.1 Purpose

The purpose of a memo is to communicate as *briefly* as possible, so that action will follow as *quickly* as possible. It cannot do this effectively unless its subject and intention are immediately obvious to the recipient.

8.1.2 The importance of memos

The memo is essential in any organisation. Messages need to be sent from one person to another; giving instructions, requesting information, confirming arrangements; a memo is often used for these functions. They may be handwritten on pre-printed memo forms or, in many organisations, may now be sent by e-mail.

The memo is a form of communication used within the organisation between employees. It is not sent to anyone outside the organisation, i.e. clients, customers, business associates.

Memos are important. As much care should be taken with their composition as with any other item of internal or external communication. For certain specific purposes, memos are usually better than telephone calls or face-to-face communication, for example:

- to transmit *exactly* the same information to several people;

- to put on record the information, policies or decisions reached at a meeting or conference;

- to confirm, as a matter of record, a decision or agreement;

- to transmit information, policies or directives to an individual.

8.1.3 Topic

A memo should contain information relating to one topic only. Do not combine messages on several topics in a single memo. We are selective in the attention we give to information and we prioritise. If more than one topic is included, there is a risk of paying attention to, and acting on, the information in one part of the memo and ignoring the rest.

Memos which are a permanent record need to be filed. Where do you file a memo which covers several topics? You either need elaborate cross-referencing and indexing, or several photocopies. Keep to the principle of *one memo for each topic*.

8.1.4 Sequencing

A memo should present information in a sequence that is easy and logical for the reader to understand (see Figure 8.1). There should be:

- an introductory sentence/paragraph stating the purpose of the memo and enabling the reader to focus his or her attention on the topic;

- the main points set out in simple direct sentences, and using numbered or bullet points. Longer memos should be set out in clear paragraphs, each dealing with a specific aspect of the topic;

- a concluding sentence/paragraph identifying what action the reader needs to take about the information, and when.

Name of organization			
MEMORANDUM			
FROM:	(name and position)	DATE:	(in full)
TO:	(name(s) and position(s))	REF:	(if relevant)
SUBJECT:	(topic heading)		

Introductory sentence, giving purpose, background information.

1. Numbered points, giving information required.
2.
3.

Concluding sentence, defining action required of receiver.

(initials of sender)

ENC. (description of enclosure(s)).

Figure 8.1 The contents of a memo.

As in Figure 8.1, all memos should:

- give date and reference number (where applicable);

- indicate sender and recipient;

- give subject headings;

- deal with each consecutive point in a separate paragraph;

- indicate clearly what action the memo requires;

- indicate where appropriate who is responsible for carrying this out.

8.1.5 Checklist

Memos require considerable care in layout, composition and style so that they are fully understood and get the right response. The following checklist will be helpful:

Memo checklist

Do

Think about the receiver(s) before you write.

Use a logical sequence for the information.

Remember KISS (**Keep It Short and Simple**).

Use an appropriate style.

Remember the 4 Cs (**Clear, Concise, Correct, Complete**).

Check that the action has been carried out.

Don't

Cover more than one topic in a memo.

Send memos outside the organisation.

Send too many memos.

Use a memo to avoid personal contact.

Write memos with poor layout or style.

8.2 Notices

Notices are like memos – they are public communication. To have them read and their message accepted, take care with their composition, layout and display.

8.2.1 Function of the notice

A notices should be used when there is a need for mass communication, or where the message it contains is either important to everyone in the organisation (as in the case of safety) or is a matter of selective interest only. Use notices if the message lends itself to visual display techniques. Notices should not be used where the message is specific to a small number of identifiable people, or when it is vital that everyone concerned has received it individually. In such cases a memo is appropriate.

8.2.2 Composition of the notice

Notices need to be brief but not abrupt. All the rules of good writing apply, especially those of brevity and clarity.

Locate notices where they will attract attention. Design them for getting that attention – use colour, bold graphics and size.

8.3 Minutes

8.3.1 Introduction

Minutes of meetings are essential. Formal committees require detailed minutes; informal meetings will usually need no more than a list of things that are to be done. The important thing about minutes is that they should be produced quickly and accurately, and show what action is required and by whom.

When chairing a meeting, help the minute taker by giving interim summaries, at the end of the discussion, of each point on the agenda. Spend a few minutes beforehand and outline the general plan of the meeting (this is invaluable to the minute taker). Explain any unfamiliar terms that may be used. Also, encourage the minute taker to interrupt the meeting if any point is not fully understood.

Where action has to be taken, deadlines should be discussed during the meeting and recorded in the minutes. It is then easy to monitor later progress. Deadlines should be firm, not vague.

Phrases like 'as soon as possible' mean different things to different people.

Minutes of any meeting should be sent to each of the participants as quickly as possible. The format should be:

- topics discussed

- votes taken;

- decisions reached.

Distributing the minutes ensures the following:

- Everyone receives the same summary of what took place. If anyone thinks they heard anything different from what is reported in the summary, they can make their views known to the secretary immediately.

- There can be no confusion as to who was assigned to do what. Names and assignments are given.

- No confusion will exist over the decisions reached and the votes taken. They will be clearly stated in writing.

- The minutes become a matter of record. They can be referred to by those who were absent, and reviewed by those who were present.

8.3.2 Writing minutes

At a meeting, the minute taker will need to ensure that a record of the proceedings is taken down. These will be written up after the meeting and will form the minutes.

Minutes follow the same order as the agenda; they must be an accurate record of what was said and agreed. They need to be written down in concise note form. Occasionally verbatim minutes may be required; these will be an exact record of everything that was said at the meeting. Often these are reproduced from a tape recording and in doing so any infelicities of language should be corrected, but the intention of the speaker should not be altered.

There are two types of minutes:

Narrative minutes

- If absent members want to check on the discussion that took place in their absence, these minutes are preferable.

- If the chairperson wants to have a record of individual members' attitudes and opinions on various issues, these minutes may be useful.

- For voluntary committees it may help members to feel that their contributions to the proceedings are valued.

- In 'political' committees (i.e. those which involve the members in impressing other people), narrative minutes can be used to convince readers that the individual who speaks (and is noted/minuted) is powerful or important.

Resolution minutes

- Such minutes reinforce the idea that the resolution is a collective decision by which all members will stand, regardless of the debate which may have preceded it.

- Such minutes are preferred by meetings that like short, succinct records rather than long reports.

8.3.3 Taking notes for minutes

The following guidelines will ensure that notes are accurate and relevant:

- Record date, time and place of meeting.

- List all members attending the meeting in alphabetical order. Note the chairperson (in brackets).

- List any apologies for absence.

- Use the agenda as the guide; give each topic a clear subheading, briefly summarise the discussion (if narrative minutes) or the resolution (if resolution minutes). Record the decision taken, the votes counted, the action to be taken and by whom.

- Do not attempt to take note of every word spoken. A *summary* of the *main* facts and arguments is needed. Listening skills and practised note-taking are essential.

- Make maximum use of schematic note layout: use spacing and indentation, and capitals for headings. Use a referencing system of numbers or letters to clearly identify each heading, subheading and points.

- When recording narrative minutes, ensure that statements are attributed to the right person. *Always* note any action to be taken by individual members.

- If there is uncertainty about any point to be recorded, ask the chairperson at the time – do not leave it until later. If the pace of the meeting prevents noting all the main points, ask members to slow down or to repeat points.

- Never record *opinion* unless strictly relevant to the resolution (in the case of narrative minutes). Never write notes from a personal point of view – an objective record is required.

After the meeting, draft the formal minutes as soon as possible. Check notes taken during the meeting against those recorded by the chairperson to make sure there is agreement on the discussion and resolutions. The minutes, once produced, should be circulated to the members who attended, absent members and anyone who may be affected by the resolutions or who is required to take some form of action.

The final minutes must follow all the rules of good writing and be clear, concise, complete and correct. Use straightforward language; avoid long words and technical jargon; use simple constructions so that the readers will easily be able to recall the decisions taken.

8.4 Manuals

8.4.1 Purpose

Manuals fall into three main categories.

- *Systems documentation manuals.* These have detailed information about the development of a piece of equipment or a particular procedure. They are usually very technical and specific, and are used as a means of communication between specialists. There are well-defined structures for such manuals.

- *Operating manuals.* These may be derived from a systems documentation manual. The objective is to tell users how to make a machine or system perform a particular function. It is this type of manual that we consider in this chapter.

- *Training manuals.* These combine the characteristics of both systems and operating manuals. They will usually contain systems information together with standard procedural instructions, coaching opportunities, troubleshooting methods and techniques of instruction.

A good manual:

- will give only the information that the users need to know with no irrelevancies;

- is easy for the users to understand from the way it is written and presented;

- is easy for the users to find the information they need through a table of contents, index, numbering of headings and cross-referencing;

- is well-organised, with effective use of headings, graphics adjacent to text, and an easy-to-read typeface.

8.4.2 Writing a manual

The technique for writing a manual is the same as for all business writing: write it clearly and concisely. We want people to absorb and understand complex instructions. So:

- Use short sentences and simple words.

- It is essential to know who the readers (users) will be.

- Aim to keep the Clarity Index at about 30–35.

- Use the active voice and an action verb to begin a sentence wherever possible.

- Number the lists if the sequence is important; otherwise use bullet points.

8.4.3 The users' (readers') needs

With manuals there is always more than one reader. Those readers will have differing needs. There are three key questions.

Who are the users?

Identify the types of user. Are they:

- new operators?

- trainers?

- installers?

- servicers?

- experienced operators?

- occasional users?

How will they use the manual?

- To learn the system from scratch?

- To remind them how to carry out an infrequently performed task?

- To cope with a fault?

- To set up a new procedure?

- To perform a function they have not previously carried out?

These are examples of the kind of questions to ask. The exact questions will depend on the subject of the manual and the particular users at whom it is aimed.

Consider also where the manual is going to be used:

- in an office?

- beside a machine?

- under a machine?

- in a training room?

- out in the pouring rain?

Environmental conditions may have an impact on the manual design.

What do they need to know?

Consider what the users already know – including the words they are likely to understand. The manual is intended to be used for practical purposes, therefore little background and no theory needs to be included. The manual is a tool for doing a job, so irrelevancies are out.

Having determined the users and their needs, think about the structure. Can all the needs be covered in one manual? It is sometimes more practical to separate out the information needed only by particular categories of user than to produce a weighty manual. Label and title it carefully, so that users can easily find the parts they want.

8.4.4 Deciding structure

The users are the most important deciding factor. The analysis of who the users are, what they are doing when referring to the manual, and what they need from it give good indicators of appropriate structure.

Every part of the manual should make sense, without reference to other sections. This does not mean eliminating cross-referencing – that is essential. For example, if the reader cannot understand what an instruction means without referring to a diagram, then put the diagram beside the instruction, or provide a fold-out diagram that can be set alongside the text.

Keep theory and practice separate. Practical instructions must remain practical – do not include a lot of background information or theory. If the theory and practice are on the same page, they should be kept in separate columns. Or put the background knowledge in separate sections, linked to the practical with extensive cross-referencing.

If the company or industry has a customary way of structuring manuals, then continue this practice. Users will already be familiar with the format and will know how to find the information they want.

Avoid the temptation to put everything into the manual just because it is available. Is the information going to be useful to the known users for their specific purposes? If not, leave it out. Or put it in an appendix, where it will not get in the readers' way as they get on with their jobs. Remember, the value of a manual is not judged by its weight.

8.4.5 The structure

Instruction manuals are different from ordinary books – people don't read them through from beginning to end. They want to be able to go straight to the particular information they need. As long as people can find what they want (which usually means having a good alphabetical index), and the manual is thoroughly cross-referenced to help the user find related topics, then we have a useful structure.

In many cases a manual will combine different types of structure; choose the one best suited to the users of that part of the manual. There is no one right basis for creating a logical structure

---

for manuals. The wide range of options for operating manuals is outlined below:

By operations

Divisions could be into sections, such as:

- Installation

- Routine Maintenance

- Fault Finding.

By functions

For example, a manual for a computer spreadsheet program might have sections such as:

- Using a Worksheet

- Creating Graphs

- Linking to Other Programs.

By level of skill or knowledge

This type of structure is often used for tutorial sections of a manual and progresses from the simple to the complex.

By user

Each section is targeted towards the needs of a particular category of user, such as:

- Operator

- Supervisor

- Engineer.

By type of information

Less common, this type of structure may involve sections such as:

- Overview

- Fault Analysis

- Standards

- Diagrams.

Alphabetically

The encyclopaedia approach is often used for reference manuals.

8.4.6 Presentation

The standard of presentation will help the readers find and use the information they need. Key points to consider are as follows:

- Operating manuals are intended to be used – covers should be strong and the binding loose-leaf for ease of alteration and amendment.

- Make headings clear and specific so they are effective signposts.

- Link graphics and text so the readers can easily relate one to the other.

- Provide a comprehensive table of contents, and ensure that the entries match the headings used in the manual itself.

- Provide a detailed index.

- Set up a numbering system for easy cross-referencing and provide for future updating. A system of chapter–section–page is best used to meet this objective, for example '3–11–5'.

- Be consistent in showing particular types of information. For example, information to be entered into a computer could always be shown in italic typeface.

- Define page size, layout and typography so that information is consistently presented and looks attractive.

- Make manuals uniform if they are going to be printed and widely distributed. Use colour coded binders for manuals for different operations so that they are quickly identified.

8.4.7 *Standard procedure instructions*

Any manual will include a number of standard procedure instructions (SPIs). In some the SPIs will form the main content.

An SPI is a written instruction, describing a procedure or process or method of operation. It is always in a standard format.

The opening of the SPI has two sections:

* a short narrative explaining the purpose of the function and its importance;

* a short narrative explaining the application of the function to that area, department, etc.

If SPIs are in narrative form they should contain as few words as possible and be direct, clear, unambiguous and functional. Commence each instruction with an imperative: 'do', 'put', 'lift', 'place', 'insert', etc. If they are in flowchart form, each step must be numbered in sequence with the narrative directly referring to that point only. Use the active voice only.

Certain basic facts should be covered in every SPI:

* subject/title

* sequence number/revision number

* date of issue

* to whom issued

* number of copies/copy number

- issued by

- authorised by

- supersedes number.

Code SPIs systematically when large numbers of procedures are involved. A good system uses letters and numbers. The letter indicates the field of application, for example:

A – sales procedures

B – accounting procedures

C – production procedures   etc.

The first number shows the function within the field:

C1 – production control

C2 – stores

C3 – procurement

C4 – maintenance   etc.

The second number subdivides the functions:

C21 – goods received

C22 – inspection of bought-out goods

C23 – stocktaking   etc.

Well constructed SPIs will contribute a great deal to the smooth operating of the function which they cover.

CHAPTER 9

Letters, faxes and e-mail

'You write with ease to show your breeding,

But easy writing's curs't hard reading'.

Sheridan

9.1 Introduction

The principles of good writing apply equally to letter writing. When you can write a good report, then good letter writing can be quickly learned. As there is much less space in a letter, carefully follow the third of the five principles – say it as clearly as you can. That implies following the same rules on use of words, length of sentences and paragraphs, correct punctuation and so on.

It is important to identify the reader – in fact, it is easier because you know to whom you are writing. You can adapt your style to their needs. However, if you receive a letter in old-fashioned pompous 'officialese' it does not mean that you have to respond similarly. Write back in a clear conversational style – show them a good example!

But beware – sometimes it is tactful to avoid part of the truth, and it may be prudent not to be too blunt. Letters may offend a reader if *too* clear, concise, simple and direct. On the other hand, excessive brevity could be rude or disturbing. So get to know your reader – watch for their reaction.

The key to good letter writing is courtesy:

- Always answer letters promptly.

- Get your correspondent's name correct – with the right spelling.

- Get their titles right.

- Be considerate and sincere.

9.2 The five 'Cs'

In letter writing, even more so than in writing reports, these five rules are invaluable. The letter writer is much closer to the reader; so these rules are even more relevant.

If you:

- recognize the importance of the relationship between *purpose, reader* and *language* and

- are prepared to be guided by the Five 'Cs'

you will have an excellent chance of achieving readability, the quality which compels a reader to go on reading, understanding and being influenced by all that has been written.

- *Be clear.* Avoid the ambiguous; use correct punctuation; use words tidily; place adjectives and adverbs in the right context.

- *Be concise.* Brevity lies in the selection and assembly of words; eliminate 'padding' caused by meaningless and hackneyed clichés, jargon and 'commercialese'!

- *Be correct.* This applies to your use of facts, figures, data, detail, information. In letter construction ensure correct grammar, punctuation and especially spelling.

- *Be complete.* Provide all the information/answers to satisfy the reader and the purpose of the letter. Also, if there are enclosures – enclose them!

- *Be courteous.* Choose and use words to create the right tone which will convey the 'image' to the reader of a warm, helpful, interested human being!

9.3 Preparation

Before beginning to write a letter, be sure:

- that you know what you want to say;

- of the sequence in which you are going to say it.

This will save time and will also give you a better chance of writing a good letter. If your letter is a reply, make certain that you have understood exactly what you have been asked and that you have gathered all the necessary facts.

A letter needs a beginning, middle and end. Think out how your letter should start. A good start, if your letter is in reply to one received, is 'Thank you for your letter of 15 April'. Certainly do not begin 'I acknowledge receipt of . . .', 'I am in receipt of . . .' or 'Further to your recent . . .'

The middle section will contain the points, answers and questions in a logical order. This needs to be thought out, in the same way as in writing a report. If it is a long letter, break it up using subheadings. Use paragraphs throughout, averaging about three or four sentences to each paragraph.

As a letter is relatively short, the end does not normally need to be a summary. A suitable final sentence might be 'I hope this has answered your questions', 'Thank you for your help', 'If you have any questions, please ring me' or something similar and friendly.

9.4 Headings

First decide whether to give the letter a heading. There are no rules as to when to use a heading, but the following will help:

- if your correspondent has already used a heading, use the same heading in your reply;

- if a heading shortens your letter;

- if you are beginning a correspondence which may lead to a sequence of letters on the subject.

If a heading is used, simply underline it or type it in bold and don't underline. Do not use all capitals – this has an aggressive look.

9.5 Hail and farewell

9.5.1 Greetings

If you are on first name terms with the reader, then address them as 'Dear Peter/Mary'. (The greeting 'Dear' is the accepted convention for address – it does not imply any affection. *Never*, in writing a business letter, use 'My dear . . .') The most usual form of address is 'Dear Mr/Mrs' (or 'Ms' if you are not sure how the lady wishes to be known).

You may not be sure if your correspondent is male or female because they have not indicated this in their letter. If they have signed '. . . Evelyn Jones', or simply 'E. Jones' then you may address them as 'Dear Evelyn Jones' – a bit coy perhaps, but safe.

If you do not know the person's name then the usual formal greeting is 'Dear Sir/Madam'. If you are writing to a government minister or official (whose name you know) then address them as

'Dear Minister' or 'Dear Under-Secretary'. If your correspondent happens to have a title, use it correctly; Sir John Smith is addressed as 'Dear Sir John'; Lord Arthur of Camelot is addressed as 'Dear Lord Arthur'.

The reason for dwelling on this topic is that first impressions are important and if you have addressed your correspondent incorrectly, they may be irritated and consequently the effectiveness of your letter may be diminished. Note that greetings also govern how you sign off (see section 9.5.2).

Often companies require letters to be addressed to them, rather than to individuals. One advantage of this is that the letter is not left unattended if the individual concerned happens to be away. Nowadays this rule tends to be relaxed and less formal. The normal form of greeting for letters addressed to organisations is 'Dear Sirs'.

9.5.2 Endings (salutations)

Two endings, 'Yours faithfully' or 'Yours sincerely' are sufficient. The first should be used after 'Dear Sir' the second after 'Dear Mr Smith' or other more personal greeting. It is simply bad form to use any Victorian style flourishes before the salutation. A sort of halfway house of 'Yours truly' with variations has crept in from American practice. It feels less formal than 'Yours faithfully' but is less warm than 'Yours sincerely'. It is rather tentative, but make your own mind up about its use.

If you wish, type the name of your organisation and your name and position underneath it. However, if the letter is written on headed notepaper, entering the firm's name is irrelevant and superfluous. Stating your position may have some point if you need to impose some authority. If you are writing to someone you know, they are aware of who you are, so your title is irrelevant.

Always sign your name. It is courteous and necessary. If a letter is worth sending it is worth reading by the writer, and a signature takes up only one more second of time.

If your signature is illegible – and most are – have your name typed beneath your signature.

If you are writing a letter for someone else, but not to be signed by them, sign your name 'for Sales Director' or 'for Chief Engineer', etc.

9.6 The parts of a letter

9.6.1 The opening paragraph

The opening paragraph should make clear the reason why the letter is being written. If it is a reply to a letter, acknowledge its receipt in the first sentence, unless there is a subject heading. So:

> *'Thank you for your letter of 10 June about the site inspection . . .'*

Do not write, unless you want to be a murderer of English:

'Your favour of 10th inst. to hand re the site inspection . . .'

If you begin:

'In reply to your letter of . . .'

continue by saying what you are doing about it:

'In reply to your letter of 10 June, we sent the parcel by registered post yesterday.'

which is perfectly natural and correct.

9.6.2 The body of the letter

The objective is to quickly bring to the mind of your correspondent the information, problem or question which you have – or should have – clear in your mind. Therefore, in writing your letter:

- be as brief as possible, but cover all the necessary points;

- cover the subject in a logical sequence;

- each subdivision of the subject should form a separate paragraph;

- sentences should be short.

You may use the first person in business letters. This means that letters beginning 'Dear Sir' will normally be written in the first person plural ('we'). Letters beginning 'Dear Mr Smith', or more informally, will either be written in the first person singular ('I'), or you can mix the first persons singular and plural.

Paragraph numbering depends on the nature of the letter. If you expect a reply dealing separately with several points mentioned in your letter, numbering the paragraphs will help in future letters. It will also help ensure that no point will be overlooked. Numbering also gives the letter orderliness and incisiveness – but only if it serves a purpose. If it does not, it may just be fussy. It is a matter of judgement.

9.6.3 The final paragraph

Letters do not usually need a closing summary. If the body of the letter has followed a logical sequence, it brings itself to a natural end. A closing, single-sentence paragraph will be useful to re-emphasise points or to sum up the letter.

For the final paragraph, do not use a stereotyped and meaningless formula. 'Awaiting the favour of your esteemed command' or 'Assuring you of our best attention at all times' and the like are capital offences!

9.6.4 Forbidden phrases

Do not use hackneyed, meaningless 'commercialese' phrases such as: 'attached please find', 'at your earliest convenience', 'the aforementioned date', 'above mentioned', 'we would be obliged', 'in due course'.

There are so many of these old clichés. Using them will certainly produce poor letters which will not communicate. Avoid them – edit them out ruthlessly.

9.7 The letter report

A short report is often more effective if presented as a letter. It is less formal and can be prepared quickly. In the format of a letter, conclusions and recommendations can be highlighted and action taken.

A letter report is usually organised into the following main sections:

* purpose of the report;

* scope of the study;

* approach – how the work was done;

* findings and analysis;

* conclusions;

* recommendations.

There is no need for a preliminary summary. The whole letter report is short, and the reader gets the entire message quickly.

In the section describing the approach, organise the content in the sequence the work was done. The sections themselves, and their relationship to each other, must support the message you are trying to give. Build up to the important information. Make it easy for the reader to get the information most needed.

An alternative method is for each section to be headed by one of the major recommendations. Then each section could contain the findings and conclusions that led to the recommendation. However, ideas may overlap, and each of the findings and conclusions may relate to more than one recommendation. It is then more appropriate to group findings, conclusions and recommendations in separate sections.

The letter report combines the organisation techniques of report writing with the more relaxed style of a letter. If you are used to writing business letters, the letter report format is easy to handle. Supporting data, by way of tables, charts, etc. included in the findings, need to be very short. Topic headings and subheadings are an essential part of getting the message across succinctly.

Think about the amount of detail, including how much you write and the extent to which you give specifics. When deciding how much detail to include, consider the reader's understanding of the subject and whether they need persuading.

It is tempting to give a detailed account of things that are particularly interesting to you, or about which you are particularly well informed. Resist that temptation. If you are going to write

---

volumes on an item, make sure it is because the reader needs the information, not because you enjoy writing it. Too much information may deceive the reader by suggesting that minor points are major.

Conversely, too little information on important points may make the reader think they are unimportant. Or, if you fail to explain an idea fully, your reader may not understand what you mean.

The choice of words also influences the emphasis of your ideas. If you feel strongly about a point of view you might say 'We are convinced . . .' A weaker expression would be 'We believe . . .' But use superlatives and statements of certainty with caution. They are often misleading.

Avoid words that convey certainty you cannot justify. We mislead the reader whenever we use words that incorrectly imply certainty. Be careful to choose the words that give the proper emphasis.

9.8 The layout of a business letter

9.8.1 Appearance

The general impression created by the layout of the letter is important. A reader will form mental pictures before a word is read. Follow house rules, where they exist, but if your organisation does not have any, the following indicators will be helpful.

- Present a neat and attractive layout

- Avoid solid 'chunks' of typing.

- Keep sentences to 10–20 words. This makes reading and understanding easy.

- Give emphasis to information of particular importance to the reader by creating separate paragraphs. These may be alphabetically or numerically referenced – or given additional attraction with an icon.

- Production must be to the highest standards.

- Ensure correct spelling – use a dictionary.

If the business letter has this type of appearance, it will attract and hold the reader's attention, and will continue to do so the more the tone of the letter appeals to him.

9.8.2 Tone and 'you' appeal

Tone has many ingredients:

- Emphasise the 'you' attitude of the letter. The 'you' attitude comprises:

  - seeing a situation from the other person's point of view;

  - sensitivity and a sincere respect for others and thus an understanding of the needs of the reader;

- the ability to communicate your empathy in words.

The 'you' attitude is not necessarily agreement. A strong 'you' attitude can be communicated even though you disagree with the other person. We do not always have to agree, but the other person does want us to express understanding and appreciate their point of view.

- Personalise the opening greeting.

- Avoid subject matter headings unless essential or to conform to house style.

- Use familiar and direct words, not commercial jargon.

- Eliminate 'hackneyed' expressions – replace them with warm meaningful language.

- Identify benefits for the reader.

- Be precise, not vague.

- Avoid the footnote: 'Dictated by . . . and signed in his absence'. Use a personal signature. Identify yourself clearly.

- Make sure that enclosures *are* enclosed.

- Use the appropriate salutation.

The letter must make sense. The essential in all communications is to be understood – and to show understanding. All this will enhance the 'you' appeal of your letter.

9.9 Special context letters

Letters which:

- answer enquiries

- acknowledge orders

- answer complaints

- collect debts

need special handling.

9.9.1 Enquiries

To answer an *enquiry*:

- Reply quickly.

- Answer every point raised.

- Open with a positive statement.

- Make it a goodwill, as well as a selling, letter.

- Emphasise benefits.

- Make the reader want to buy – give reasons for taking immediate action.

And most importantly:

- Make it easy to take that action.

9.9.2 Acknowledgement

To acknowledge an *order*:

- Thank the customer.

- Welcome a new customer warmly.

- Get it right! Confirm terms, quantities, delivery, discounts, special conditions.

- Check incomplete orders immediately. Avoid implied criticism.

When unable to complete the order:

- Give good news first.

- Apologise for mistakes.

- Never pass the blame to someone else.

9.9.3 Complaints

When answering a *complaint*:

- Investigate.

- Reply quickly – if the investigation is not complete, say so.

- Promise a further reply within seven days.

- Be friendly and courteous, even if the letter of complaint is not.

- If it is your mistake, apologise quickly.

- Explain – briefly if the complaint is justified, fully if it is not.

- Do not pass the blame to someone else.

- If an item under complaint is to be replaced, or money refunded, do not stress your company's generosity.

- Give good news quickly.

- Thank the complainant for drawing your attention to the problem.

- Re-establish confidence by reselling goods or services.

Never use expressions such as:

It is not our policy . . .	(patronising)
We cannot understand . . .	(patronising)
We are surprised . . .	(patronising)
We cannot trace your previous communication . . .	('you are a liar')
Your claim . . .	('you are a liar')
You state . . .	('you are a liar')
You failed to read the instructions . . .	('you are a fool')
Our records prove . . .	('you are a liar')
You overlooked our terms . . .	('you are a fool')

As I told you before . . .	('you are a fool')
You really cannot expect us . . .	(patronising)
We should have thought . . .	(patronising)
It seems obvious to us . . .	(patronising)
Our files show . . .	('you are a fool')
In the circumstances we shall allow . . .	(patronising)

This sort of high-handed dismissal of the complaint is guaranteed to offend, annoy, even disgust. You will certainly lose a customer – you may even get involved in a law suit.

Never use such expressions.

9.9.4 Debt collection

If the debt is seriously overdue investigate whether:

- the customer is deliberately paying slowly to obtain extended credit;

- the customer has a grievance;

- the customer does not pay because he is temporarily short of money;

- the customer cannot pay.

If there is a grievance, settle that first. Collection will then follow easily.

If a customer cannot pay, do not waste your time. Either write it off as a bad debt or take legal action.

If the customer does not pay because he is temporarily short of money, offer a payment plan.

If the customer is deliberately paying slowly, write a letter using humour, pride, face-saving, urgency, fair play, fear – or a combination of these. Debt collecting is an onerous task. The 'you' appeal of any letter you write will be an important factor in your debt collection success.

9.10 Faxes and e-mails

Fax and e-mail are simply different methods of transmission of the written word. Both are virtually instantaneous – which raises some problems. Both are intensive and generate a level of urgency that a letter falling on your desk does not.

Nevertheless, in spite of urgency it is not necessary to abandon the letter writing rules that we follow with 'snail mail'.

9.10.1 Fax

To be effective a fax should be short – yards of fax paper are a deterrent to reading. Always head a fax with the subject and the addressee's name, rather like a memo. It is not necessary to set out the name and address at the top left.

The greeting, body of the letter and salutation should follow the usual letter writing rules. However, the fax format does give you the opportunity to practise brevity and to move straight to the point of the communication. Be brief, but not terse, and remain courteous.

The fax format provides an ideal opportunity to cut out all the outdated 'commercialese' so often to be found in business letters.

9.10.2 E-mail

Business communication is about getting your message across clearly and in a professional manner. Writing letters and sending them by e-mail is no different. But people, who are normally competent and confident letter writers somehow find themselves hesitant when it comes to business e-mail. This is probably because it is very hard to find the right tone – it is too easy to drop into the casual conversational mode.

Resist this: write e-mail letters as you would write a normal business letter and then ask yourself: 'How would I feel if I received this message?'

E-mail may be global but it has not yet broken down international business etiquette barriers, so start formally with 'Dear Mr X' which is much better than 'Hi there!' Correct spelling and good grammar are essential – jokes and chatroom shorthand are out. Doing business by e-mail can be a bit impersonal – you need to know your reader exists in the real world! Making contact by phone as well is a good way to build your relationship. Reply to e-mails promptly. A swift 'I'll get back to you' is better than silence.

Enclosures

Add confidentiality or security notices to your e-mails: if you are not sure who may read them – be safe rather than sorry. Do not send large attachments: 'snail mail' may be better if there is time.

Do not send any '.exe' files as attachments unless you are very well-known to the recipient. Any person receiving one of these from a stranger will automatically suspect a virus and be extremely annoyed!

You can place orders, present proposals and finalise contracts via e-mail, but anything requiring a signature will still need a letter, fax or face-to-face meeting.

E-mail is a great form of direct marketing, but be very careful that your message does not come over as 'spam' (the e-mail equivalent of junk mail).

9.11 Summary

In business writing, the reader must understand what you are saying, so what you write must be simple, clear and to the point – stick to straightforward, uncluttered English.

Think about what you are going to write before you write it. Make notes and prepare. Be absolutely clear in your mind what you wish to say and how you intend to say it.

All business writing should be *logical*, *truthful*, *helpful* (where possible) and to the point. Remember always:

$$Clarity + Simplicity = Efficiency$$

CHAPTER 10

Endpiece

'The end of this day's business'

Shakespeare, *Julius Caesar*

Congratulations – you've got to the end of the book. It's now time for recapitulation (oops – a long word!).

In any writing, if you want to ensure that your meaning will stick, it's a good idea to 'tell them again'. We started this book with describing what you have to do before you undertake any serious writing. This process of identifying in your mind why you are writing, and who you are writing for, is so valuable that you omit it at your peril. Indeed, if you do, you will soon be in a real mess, and the end result is also likely to be a muddle, which will do your credibility no good at all.

Once you have decided why and who, you have to think about what: what you are going to tell them – that means your facts, figures and so on, your material. We talked about various ways of getting this together – deciding what is relevant and what to discard (hard sometimes), and how to organise it. Good business writing should be clear and well structured, so that the reader has no difficulty following the argument.

The secret of effective business writing lies in the clarity of expression. Using clear familiar words, short sentences, the active voice and short one-topic paragraphs will all help to make your writing easy to understand at first reading. Readability is the key factor. If your writing is dense and difficult your readers will soon give up – they haven't the time nor the inclination to try to understand your turgid prose. We outlined a method of measuring readability – use this and adjust your writing to achieve a reasonable clarity index that will suit the audience for whom you are writing. They will appreciate your care.

We all know how to write – we've been taught, we've learned and we've read this book. But sometimes getting started is difficult as is deciding the right style to use. This is where the preparation, the thinking before writing clicks in. We all get 'writer's block' at times, but this need not be a traumatic situation. You have done the creative bit, assembled all your material, now all you have to do is get it down on paper. And if you have followed our 'paragraph option' advice, you've done half your writing already. Sounds easier than it is? No, it is easier than you think.

Your real problem is the words – there are so many and they are tricky! Don't be seduced into purple prose – you are not writing a novel, this is business writing. Use plain, simple, everyday words; your readers will appreciate it. They will be able to understand your language without having to use a dictionary. And put your words into short grammatical sentences – not too long, not too short. Vary them as we have done in this book. Try to get a conversational pattern into your writing. A sentence should contain a single idea, or at most (in a compound sentence) two ideas. Work out your idea in combining your sentences into paragraphs. Again not too long, the paragraph should work around the development of the same idea. Remember: new idea, new paragraph. But look at your writing in print – if you have 40 lines of text as a single paragraph, that is too much. Chop it up. By the way, nothing says that you can't have a single line paragraph, or a single word sentence, if it is appropriate.

When you have written your piece, you need to revise and edit it. Don't try and do this as you go along, it isn't going to work. To create a really good piece of writing that gets its message across clearly and concisely, you will need to revise a lot. Move items around to create a logical structure. Your writing will also be 100% better if you chop out anything between 30 and 50% of what you have written. Cut out unnecessary words and whole sentences

---

and paragraphs – tighten it up. Look at the words you have used – are they right? can you use simpler ones? Do you really need that paragraph? Is that piece of information really necessary? does it add anything useful? This process of ruthless editing is what makes an ordinary piece of writing good. Think of your purpose and your reader – edit to achieve your goal. Don't let the idea of editing inhibit you as you write. Just get it down on paper. To get your ideas from your brain into the reader's, the words have to get onto the page. As you write them, try to express the ideas as clearly as you can. Then edit to ensure that your message gets across clearly and directly.

The art of business letter writing is one which can also be learned. The basic principles are essentially the same as for any other business writing, but there is one big advantage – generally you know who the reader is. Also letters tend to be shorter, dealing mostly with a single specific subject. Nevertheless, we need to organise our material so as to present it to the reader in a coherent way, and so that what you want to say is quickly understood. There is a great temptation to ramble in a letter – resist this and subject your letters to the same searching process of editing as for other business writing. To the four general rules of writing – be clear, be concise, be correct and be complete – may be added a fifth – be courteous. Courtesy is always important, but never more so than in letter writing when you are addressing an individual.

Much of the advice that has been given in this book may appear to be self-evident. That is true to some extent. But it's remarkable how often, when faced with a difficult writing job, all our common sense disappears. We strive to impress, we are pompous and obscure, we forget the basic rules. Now that you have read and absorbed the simple ideas that are in this book, hopefully you will be able to follow the guidelines and produce . . .

Good writing!

APPENDIX 1

Reference works

General

The following books are useful references and sources of inspiration for any writer. The list could be extended almost indefinitely, but these titles are relevant for the users of this book.

Tony Buzan, *Use Your Head (Mind Maps)*, BBC Publications.

Michael David (ed.), *Manuals That Work*, Kogan Page.

The Economist, *Pocket Style Book*, The Economist.

Rudolph Flesch, *The Art of Readable Writing*, Harper & Row.

H. W. Fowler, *Modern English Usage*, Oxford University Press.

Sir Ernest Gowers, *The Complete Plain Words*, Penguin.

Eric Partridge, *Usage and Abusage*, Hamish Hamilton.

Jan Venolia, *Write Right*, David & Charles.

Dictionaries

If in doubt about a word, use a dictionary! Which dictionary you use is a matter of personal choice.

Here are some suggestions:

BBC English Dictionary (HarperCollins)
The standard reference for the worldwide language as used by the BBC for home and World Service broadcasts.

The Concise Oxford Dictionary
Oxford dictionaries are widely regarded as the definitive editions. The Concise Edition provides a halfway house between the full version (massive in size), and the Pocket Editions which do not always contain the unusual words you are seeking.

Harrap's English Spelling
Does not give the meanings of words, only their spelling, but does list words in the ways they are commonly misspelled so that you can find a word even when you do not know how to spell it correctly.

Longmans Dictionary of Business English
Very useful for business terminology, especially banking, insurance and commerce.

Longmans Dictionary of Contemporary English

This has several features which distinguish it from dictionaries in the Oxford series:

- a focus on contemporary words;
- definitions using a limited 2,000-word vocabulary – this avoids having to look up additional meanings to find out the meaning of the word you originally looked up!
- lots of examples of the words in use.

Oxford Advanced Learners Dictionary

Good on etymology and sources of first use. Good, plain and straightforward definitions.

Oxford Student Dictionary

A useful, rather more compact Concise Edition, with fewer words and shorter definitions.

Websters 9th New Collegiate Dictionary (Merriam-Webster)
Useful for the American idiom.

You may also find it useful to have a Thesaurus or a dictionary of synonyms and antonyms.

Dictionaries and reference books are expensive and are constantly being revised. There is no real harm in not using the very latest edition. The words themselves won't change! However, if you decide to buy a new book, get the latest edition. Word *meanings* in contemporary usage do change; forewarned is better than sounding foolish.

APPENDIX 2

The rules of spelling

These are the main spelling rules, in the British (as opposed to the American) convention. They are sometimes odd, but they do have a certain logic. And words *look* wrong if spelled incorrectly. If in doubt Appendix 3 may help.

The rules	Examples
Words of one syllable ending in a single consonant preceded by a single vowel double the consonant when affixing a suffix.	dim, dimmed blot, blotted; sin, sinned sad, sadden
Words of more than one syllable, ending in a single consonant preceded by a single vowel, if the accent is on the final syllable also double the consonant before a suffix.	compel, compelling rebut, rebutted infer, inferred

The consonant is not doubled if the word ends in two consonants	gild, gilded bowl, bowled hard, harden
or if it has a double vowel	feast, feasting exceed, exceeded
or when the accent is not on the last syllable.	benefit, benefited limit, limited fillet, filleted
Whatever the position of the accent, a final letter *l* is almost invariably doubled	travel, traveller cancel, cancelled jewel, jeweller
but a single letter *l* is not doubled before -*ish, -ism, -ist, -ment*	devilish socialism nationalist fulfilment
and a word ending with a double letter *l* usually retains the *ll* before -*ness*.	illness dullness fullness
Adverbs formed by adding -*ly* to adjectives ending in -*l* or -*ll* always keep the *ll*.	beautiful, beautifully frugal, frugally full, fully

Words ending in *n* retain it when adding *-ness*.	thinness meanness sternness
A double *n* also comes in words formed by adding the prefix *un-*, *en-* or *in-* to words beginning with *n*.	necessary, unnecessary noble, ennoble numerable, innumerable
Double consonants also occur when *il-*, *ir-* or *im-* is added as a prefix.	legal, illegal regular, irregular modest, immodest
Words ending in a silent *e* drop the *e* before a suffix beginning with a vowel, but not before a suffix beginning with a consonant.	move, movable *but* movement; excite, exciting, *but* excitement
But there are some exceptions to preserve the soft sound.	singe *becomes* singeing notice *becomes* noticeable advantage *becomes* advantageous

Words ending in *y* preceded by a consonant change *y* to *i* before a suffix beginning with any letter except *i*.	cry, cried, *but* crying reply, replied, *but* replying carry, carried, *but* carrying
In words containing *ei* or *ie* with the sound *ee*, *i* comes before *e* except after *c*.	believe, retrieve, niece, *but* receive, perceive, ceiling
When the rule is broken, as in *ancient*, *sufficient* and similar words, the *ci* almost invariably gives the sound of *sh*. Exceptions to be noted are:	seize weird weir counterfeit

Even though these are complex, most writers manage them without too much difficulty. But if in doubt don't trust your instinct, some help is on the next page, or there is always the spelling dictionary. The American convention does simplify the spelling of some words, notably the 'ou' form, e.g. fav*ou*r, fav*o*r. There is nothing *wrong* with American spelling, but if you choose to use it, be consistent. Also, to a British reader it may 'look strange', and this can create a bias against your writing.

APPENDIX 3

Some commonly misspelled words

Refer to this list when you are not sure how to spell a word – it is likely to be included here. Keep using this list – you will find that you have become a good speller!

absence	anxiety	benefited	completely
accidentally	apparent	beneficial	conscientious
accommodate	appearance	breathe	conscious
achieved	appropriate	budgeted	consistent
acknowledge	Arctic	business	convenience
acquainted	argument	ceiling	courteous
addresses	arrangements	certain	courtesy
aerial	ascend	choice	criticism
aggravate	athletic	clothes	deceive
aggregate	atrocious	college	decision
agreeable	automation	colleagues	definite
all right	awful	coming	desirable
amateur	bachelor	committee	desperate
analysis	beginning	comparative	disappeared
Antarctic	believed	competent	disappointed

disastrous
discipline
dissatisfied
efficiency
eighth
eliminated
embarrassed
emphasise (-ize)
enthusiasm
equipped
especially
essential
exaggerated
excellent
exercise
exhausted
existence
expenses
experience
extremely
familiar
feasibility
February
financial
foreign
friend
fulfil
fulfilled
gauge
genius
government
grammar
grievance
guard
guardian

handkerchief
height
heroes
honorary
humorous
hurriedly
hypocrisy
imagination
immediately
immigrate
incidentally
independent
influential
intelligence
interrupt
irresistible
knowledge
liaison
literature
livelihood
lose
losing
lying
maintenance
marriage
medicine
Mediterranean
miniature
minutes
mischievous
murmur
necessary
negotiate
niece
noticeable

occasional
occasionally
occurred
occurrence
omitted
omission
opinion
originally
parallel
parliament
pastime
permanent
permissible
perseverance
personnel
physical
planning
pleasant
possesses
preceding
preference
prejudice
preliminary
prestige
privilege
procedure
proceeds
professional
professor
pronunciation
proprietary
psychology
questionnaire
quiet
really

received
recognize
recommended
referred
relieved
repetition
restaurant
rhythmic
scarcely
secretaries
seize
sentence
separate
severely
shining
similar
sincerely
statutory
successfully
supersede
suppression
surprising
synonymous
tendency
tragedy
transferred
twelfth
unconscious
undoubtedly
unnecessary
until
usually
valuable
Wednesday
woollen

APPENDIX 4

Words often confused and misused

English is a language rich in similar sounding (but differently spelled) words. The different spelling has a different meaning. Also one word often has several meanings. Here are some common stumbling blocks. Use the right word for your context, or run the risk of appearing illiterate, ignorant, uneducated or worse – stupid!

Accent: to stress or emphasise; a regional manner of speaking.
Assent: to agree; agreement.

Accept: to receive, to give an affirmative answer to.
Except: to exclude; to leave out; to omit.

Access: admittance or admission.
Excess: surplus or more than necessary.

Adapt: to accustom oneself to a situation.

Adept: proficient or competent in performing a task.

Adopt: to take by choice. to put into practice.

Advice: counsel; a recommendation (noun).

Advise: to suggest; to recommend (verb).

Affect: to influence (verb).

Effect: result or consequence (noun).

Effect: to bring about (verb).

All ready: prepared.

Already: previously.

Allusion: a reference to something familiar.

Illusion: an image of an object; a false impression.

Delusion: a false belief.

Among: refers to three or more.

Between: refers to two only.

Amount: quantity without reference to individual units.

Number: a total of counted units.

Anxious: upset; concerned about a serious occurrence.

Eager: very desirous; anticipating a favourable event.

Anyone: any person in general.

Any one: a specific person or item.

Assay: to evaluate.

Essay: to try or attempt.

Essay: a literary composition.

Balance: as an accounting term, an amount owed or a difference between debit and credit sums.

Remainder: that which is left over; a surplus.

Beside: by the side of.

Besides: in addition to.

Biannually: two times a year.

Biennially: every two years.

Can: refers to ability or capability.

May: refers to permission.

Callous: not sympathetic; hardened.

Callus: hardened area of skin.

Canvas: a coarse type of cloth.

Canvass: to solicit; survey.

Cannon: large gun.

Canon: a law; church official.

Capital: a seat of government; money invested; a form of a letter.

Capitol: a government building (US usage).

Cease: to halt or stop.

Seize: to grasp or take possession.

Censer: an incense pot.

Censor: a critic.

Sensor: an electronic device.

Censure: to find fault with or to blame.

Criticise: to evaluate; to examine.

Cereal: any grain.

Serial: arranged in successive order.

Cite: to quote from a source.

Sight: act of seeing; object or scene observed.

Site: a place, such as 'building site'.

Coarse: composed of large particles; unrefined.

Course: a direction of progress or a series of studies.

Collision: a clashing of objects.

Collusion: a conspiracy or fraud.

Command: to direct or order; an order.

Commend: to praise or laud.

Complacent: satisfied, smug.

Complaisant: obliging.

Complement: that which completes or supplements; a crew.

Compliment: flattery or praise.

Complimentary: something given freely.

Confidant: one who may be confided in.

Confident: positive or sure.

Consensus of opinion: redundant – *consensus* means 'general opinion'.

Contact: meeting of surfaces – frequently misused as a verb to mean 'to ask', 'to call', 'to consult' or 'to inform'.

Continual: taking place in close succession; frequently repeated.

Continuous: no break or let-up.

Council: an assembly of persons.

Counsel: to advise; advice; an attorney (US usage).

Consul: a resident representative of a foreign state.

Councillor: a member of a council.

Counsellor: a lawyer or adviser.

Core: a centre.

Corps: a body of troops; a group of persons in association.

Corpse: a dead body.

Credible: believable or acceptable.

Creditable: praiseworthy or meritorious.

Credulous: gullible.

Critic: one who evaluates.

Critique: an analytical examination of.

Criticism: an evaluation.

Currant: fruit.

Current: timely; motion of air or water.

Data / Criteria / Phenomena: the plural forms of *datum, criterion* and *phenomenon*. Sometimes used as singular, collective nouns.

Deceased: dead.

Diseased: infected.

Decent: correct; proper.

Descent: going from high to low.

Dissent: disagreement.

Decree: a proclamation of law.

Degree: difference in grade; an academic award.

Defer: to delay or put off.

Differ: to disagree.

Deference: respect.

Difference: unlikeness.

Deprecate: to express disapproval of.

Depreciate: to lessen in value because of use and/or time; to belittle.

Desert: a reward or punishment.

Desert: to abandon.

Desert: a barren geographical area.

Dessert: a course at the end of a meal.

Different from / Different than: either may be used.

Differ from: to stand apart because of unlikeness.

Differ with: to disagree.

Disapprove: not to accept.

Disprove: to prove wrong.

Disburse: to make payments; to allot.

Disperse: to scatter.

Discomfit: to frustrate; to disconcert (verb).

Discomfort: distress; not comfortable (noun).

Discreet: prudent; good judgement in conduct.

Discrete: separate entity; individual.

Disinterested: neutral; not biased.

Uninterested: not concerned with; lacking interest.

Disorganised: disordered.

Unorganised: not organised or planned.

Dual. double or two.

Duel: a contest between two antagonists.

Each other: refers to two.

One another: refers to more than two.

Either / Neither: refers to one or the other of two – with 'either' use 'or'; with 'neither' use 'nor'.

Elicit: to draw forth, usually a comment.

Illicit: unlawful; illegal.

Eligible: acceptable; approved.

Illegible: impossible to read or decipher.

Elusive: difficult to catch.

Illusive: deceptive.

Emerge: to come out.

Immerge: to plunge into, immerse.

*Emigrat*e: to travel out of one country to live in another.

Immigrate: to come into a country.

Migrate: to travel from place to place periodically.

Eminent: outstanding; prominent.

Imminent: impending, very near, or threatening.

Immanent: inherent.

Envelope: container for a communication.

Envelop: to surround, cover over or enfold.

Erotic: sexually arousing.

Erratic: unpredictable, irregular.

Exotic: foreign.

Esoteric: of interest only to a select few.

Exceptional: much better than average; superior.

Exceptionable: likely to cause objection; objectionable.

Expansive: capable of extension or expansion.

Expensive: costly.

Extant: living or in existence.

Extent: an area or a measure.

Extinct: no longer living or existing.

Distinct: clear, sharply defined.

Facet: a small surface of a cut gem stone; aspect of an object or situation.

Faucet: a tap (generally US usage).

Facilitate: to make easier.

Felicitate: to greet or congratulate.

Faint: to lose consciousness (verb); feeble, weak (adjective).

Feint: to pretend or simulate; a deceptive movement.

Farther: refers to geographical or linear distance.

Further: more; in addition to.

Fate: destiny.

Fete: to honour or celebrate (verb); a party (noun).

Feat: an act of unusual skill.

Flair: natural ability.

Flare: a signal rocket; a blazing up of a fire.

Formally: according to convention.

Formerly: previously.

Freeze: to turn solid because of low temperatures.

Frieze: ornamentation along the top edge of a wall, sometimes on hung fabric.

Genius: unusual and outstanding ability.

Genus: a grouping or classification, usually on a biological basis.

Hale: free from defect, healthy.

Hail. precipitation that has frozen.

Hail: to greet or call out.

Healthful: giving or contributing to health.

Healthy: having health.

Hoard: to collect and keep; a hidden supply.

Horde: a huge crowd.

Holistic: the entirety.

Wholly: entirely; completely.

Human: pertaining to man.

Humane: kindly, considerate.

Immunity: safety from infection; exemption from regulation.

Impunity: freedom or exemption from punishment.

Imply: to hint at or to allude to in speaking or writing.

Infer: to draw a conclusion from what has been said or written.

In: indicates location within.

Into: indicates movement to a location within.

Incite: to stir up.

Insight: keen understanding; intuition.

Incredible: extraordinary; unbelievable.

Incredulous: sceptical; not believing.

Indignant: angry.

Indigenous: native to an area or country.

Indigent: needy; poor.

Ingenious: clever, resourceful.

Ingenuous: frank, honest, free from guile.

Its: a possessive singular pronoun.

It's: a contraction for 'it is'.

Later: refers to time – the comparative form of *late*.

Latter: refers to the second named of two.

Learn: to acquire knowledge.

Teach: to impart knowledge.

Less: smaller quantity than, without reference to units.

Fewer: a smaller total of units.

Let: to permit.

Leave: to go away from; to abandon.

Lie, lay, lain: to recline.

Lay, laid, laid. to place.

Likely: probable.

Liable: legally responsible.

Apt: quick to learn; inclined; relevant.

Load: a burden; a pack.

Lode: a vein of ore.

Loath: reluctant; unwilling.

Loathe: to hate; to despise; to detest.

Lose: to cease having.

Loose: not fastened or attached; to set free.

Magnate: a tycoon; important official.

Magnet: a device that attracts metal.

Marital: used in reference to marriage.

Martial: pertaining to military affairs.

Marshal: an official; to arrange.

Maybe: perhaps (adverb).

May be: indicates possibility (verb).

Medal: a badge of honour.

Mettle: spirit or temperament.

Metal: a mineral substance.

Meddle: to interfere.

Miner: an underground labourer or worker.

Minor: one who has not attained legal age; of little importance.

Moral: a principle, maxim or lesson (noun); ethical (adjective).

Morale: a state of mind or psychological outlook (noun).

Nice: pleasant, agreeable; finely drawn, subtle – as in 'nice distinction'.

Notable: distinguished.

Notorious: unfavourably known.

Observance: following or respecting a custom or regulation.

Observation: act of seeing; casual remark.

Oral: by word of mouth.

Verbal: communication in words whether oral or written.

Ordinance: a local law.

Ordnance: military weapons; munitions.

Peak: top of a hill or mountain; topmost point.

Peek: a quick look through a small opening.

Pique: irritation. annoyance.

Peal: sound of a bell.

Peel: to strip off.

Per cent: should be used after a numeral (*20 per cent*).

Percentage: for quantity or where numerals are not used (a larger
   percentage).

Persecute: to subject to harsh or unjust treatment.

Prosecute: to bring legal action against.

Personal: private; not public or general.

Personnel: the staff of an organisation.

Plaintiff: the complaining party in a lawsuit.

Plaintive: sorrowful; mournful.

Plane: to make smooth; a tool; a surface.

Plain: area of level or treeless country; obvious, undecorated.

Practical. not theoretical; useful, pragmatic.

Practicable: can be put into practice (not used in reference to people).

Precedence: priority.

Precedents: cases that have already occurred.

Proceed: to begin; to move; to advance.

Precede: to go before.

Principal: of primary importance (adjective); head of a school; original sum; chief or official.

Principle: a fundamental truth.

Provided: on condition; supplied.

Providing: supplying.

Quite: almost; entirely; positively.

Quiet: without noise.

Recent: newly created or developed; near past in time.

Resent: to feel indignant.

Respectfully: with respect or deference.

Respectively: in order named.

Resume: to begin again.

Résumé: a summing up; a CV (US usage).

Rise: to move upward; to ascend (rise, rose, risen).

Raise: to elevate; pick up (raise, raised, raised).

Salvage: to save (verb); material saved from a fire, shipwreck, etc. (noun).

Selvage: edge of cloth.

Sit: to be seated.

Set: to put in position (set, set, set).

Sometime: at one time or another.

Sometimes: occasionally.

Stationary: not moving; fixed.

Stationery: writing paper or writing materials.

Statue: a carved or moulded three-dimensional reproduction.

Stature: height of a person; reputation.

Statute: a law.

Straight: direct; uninterrupted; not crooked.

Strait: narrow strip connecting two bodies of water; a distressing situation.

Than: used in comparison (conjunction): 'Joe is taller than Tom'.

Then: relating to time (adverb): 'First he ran; then he jumped'.

Their: belonging to them (possessive of *they*).

There: in that place (adverb).

They're: a contraction of the two words *they are*.

To: preposition: 'to the store'.

Too: adverb: 'too cold'.

Two: number: 'two apples'.

Veracity: truthfulness.

Voracity: ravenousness; greed.

Vice: wickedness.

Vise: a clamp.

Waive: to give up; relinquish.

Wave: swell of water; a gesture.

Weather: climate or atmosphere.

Whether: an alternative.

Who's: a contraction of the two words *who is*.

Whose: possessive of *who*.

Your: a pronoun.

You're: a contraction of the two words *you are*.

APPENDIX 5

Foreign words and phrases

Some writers use the occasional foreign word or phrase or 'Latin tag' for effect. It is a bit pretentious, so avoid these unless you are absolutely certain your reader will understand them. Most people have seen but understand very few of them. We would enter a caveat contra their use. Inter alia, the hoi polloi will not understand them. They are de trop and verboten.

ab initio	from the beginning
ad hoc	for this particular purpose; specially.
alter ego	other self; intimate friend
à propos	about; concerning
caveat	warning, proviso

contra	against
de rigeur	required (by custom or etiquette)
de trop	not wanted, unwelcome
et al	and others
ergo	therefore
ex cathedra	authoritatively
ex gratia (e.g.)	freely given; voluntary (common usage: for example)
faux pas	mistake; slip (especially against social convention)
hoi polloi	the majority; the rabble; the common people
id est (i.e.)	it, or (here it) is
inter alia (i.a.)	among other things
ipso facto	thereby
locum tenens	deputy (especially for a doctor or clergyman)
mutatis mutandis	making corresponding adjustments as appropriate
nom de guerre	alias; pen name
non sequitur	not following logically
obiter dictum	incidental remark

per annum	each year
per se	by or in itself; intrinsically
prima facie	a first sight; on the first impression
quid pro quo	an exchange; something given as compensation
quod vide (q.v.)	which see: referring to something already written
sic	so thus; drawing attention to the form of quoted or copied words
verboten	forbidden
vis-à-vis	facing one another; opposite to
viz.	that is to say; in other words

Some Latin abbreviations are in common use and are acceptable. Examples are: *etc.* (*etcetera* – and so on); *e.g.* (*exampli gratia* – for example); *i.e.* (*id est* – that is); *ibid.* (*ibidem* – in the same place); *pas.* (*passim* – throughout); *c.* or *ca.* (*circa* – about, used in giving dates).

APPENDIX 6

Glossary of grammar

The following definitions are provided for reference. The list is not complete; it does, however, include most common terms. We have not attempted to explain the rules of grammar or punctuation.

The parts of speech

Adjective

Modifies a noun or pronoun by describing
or qualifying it: *favourable* decision

Adverb

Modifies a verb by describing or
qualifying its action: *suddenly* realised

May also modify an adjective: *badly* damaged

---

or another adverb:	*very* highly trained
Adverbs usually end with '*-ly*':	*easily*
but not always:	*soon*
Not all words ending in '*-ly*' are adverbs	*lovely*: an adjective

Conjunction

Also called 'connective'. Connects words or complete ideas. There are three kinds:	
Coordinate:	*and, but, or, nor, for*
connects words or ideas of the same grammatical function:	The manager *and* the foreman.
Subordinate:	*although, as, unless*
connects a phrase or subordinate clause to a main clause by showing some relationship between them:	There have been fewer errors *since* the change.
Correlative:	*either–or; neither–nor; both–and; not only–but*
connects pairs and must always appear in the sentence as pairs.	

Interjection

An exclamation, in a sentence, serving no grammatical function:	*Oh*, that's not true. He was, *alas*, late again.

Noun

The name of any object:	*computer*
idea:	*truth*
process:	*designing*
condition:	*illness*

Proper nouns are capitalised, e.g. names of people, places, organisations or products. Subjects of sentences and clauses are always nouns. The form of the noun does not change to show its grammatical function; this is shown by its position in the sentence.

Preposition

Connects a noun (or word functioning as a noun) with some other part of the same

sentence. Usually it describes place:	*on* the desk
or time:	*before* the concert

Pronoun

Substitutes for a noun, phrase or clause:	he posted it to *them*

The form usually changes to describe the noun it stands for in terms of *number*, *gender* and *case*.

Verb

The action word. Every sentence or clause must contain one. It tells what the subject (a noun or pronoun) is or does. The verb may be:

transitive – requires an object; or

intransitive – complete without an object.

The form of the verb, its 'conjugations', usually changes to tell five other things about the action it describes:

1. *Number:* singular or plural

2. *Person:* I, you, he, she, it, they

3. *Tense:* past, present, future

4. *Voice:* whether the subject performs the action (active) or receives it (passive)

5. Mood:

   fact: indicative mood – most commonly used: You are here.

   command: imperative mood: Be here.

   contrary to fact: subjunctive mood: If you were here.

Other language terms

Appositive   A word or phrase placed next to another to explain or enlarge the meaning of the other.

Article   There are only three articles in English: *a* and *an* (indefinite articles); and *the* (definite article). Because they modify nouns, they are adjectives.

Auxiliary verb   (Also called a 'helping verb'.) Some form of the verb 'to be' in front of another verb, used to change its tense, voice or mood.

Complex sentence   A sentence containing one independent clause and one or more dependent (subordinate) clauses.

Compound sentence   A sentence containing two or more independent clauses, joined by a comma and a co-ordinate conjunction.

Compound-complex sentence   As its name implies, this contains both kinds of sentence described above.

Conjunctive adverb   *However, therefore, nevertheless*, connect independent clauses as conjunctions. They also modify the verb in the clause, thus they become adverbs. They help the reader *see* some special relationship between the clauses – such as cause and effect (I think, *therefore* I am).

Coordinate clauses	The two independent clauses of a compound sentence, joined by a comma and a coordinate conjunction (*and, but, or, nor, for, yet*).
Case	The form of a pronoun that tells whether it is used in a sentence as the subject (nominative), an object (accusative) or possessor (possessive). Nouns change form only for the possessive (by adding -*'s*).
Clause	A group of words that has a subject and a verb. It may be a whole sentence or part of a sentence.
	There are two main kinds:
	Independent clause – can stand alone and be a complete sentence without the help of another clause.
	Dependent clause ('subordinate' clause) – adds to an independent clause and depends on it for meaning.
Cliché	A group of words used as a common expression. The same idea can *always* be expressed without a cliché. Avoid them.

Colloquial	Common, informal, language. Has neither the heaviness of formal vocabulary nor the distasteful tone of slang. It is between the two, and is the best kind of language for most business writing.
Dangling modifier	A word or phrase that does not properly modify the part of the sentence the writer intended. Most common are dangling participles and pronouns. Take care to avoid such danglers – although the writer knows what the relationship should be, he or she might not notice if the words do not create precisely the intended meaning. (For example: 'Being old and dog-eared, I was able to buy the book for 50 pence.' Who was 'old and dog-eared', you or the book?)
Definite article	'*The*' is the only definite article in English, so called because it specifies a particular thing.
Direct object	The noun or pronoun that receives the action of a transitive verb. It may also be a phrase or clause acting as a noun.
Gender	The form of a pronoun that tells the sex of the noun (person) that it stands for (*he*, *she*, *it*).

Gerund	A verb used as a noun. It always ends with '*-ing*'. It may be a subject or an object.
Idiom	A commonly accepted term that does not follow rules of the language, or may even violate them. Prepositions are most often used idiomatically.
Imperative	The form (mood) of a verb which denotes command.
Indefinite article	'*A*' and '*an*' are the only indefinite articles in English. They do not specify a particular thing, as opposed to the definite article, which does.
Independent clause	A group of words having a subject and verb, capable of standing alone as a sentence without the help of any other words.
Indicative	The most common form (mood) of verbs, denoting that the action is fact.
Indirect object	A second object of some transitive verbs, other than the direct object, usually denoting the person or thing indirectly affected by the action of that verb.
Infinitive	The 'to be' form of any verb.
Intransitive verb	One that does not need an object to complete its meaning. All passive voice verbs are

intransitive; their subject is the word that would be the direct object of a transitive verb in the active voice.

Jargon   The specialised language of a particular profession, a kind of shorthand, expressing complex ideas in few words. It has a major disadvantage: only those in that profession can understand it. A good rule is: if an idea can be expressed in ordinary language, using the same or almost the same number of words, do not use any specialised jargon.

Metaphor   A group of words that implies a comparison to something else, usually to create a vivid image. Metaphors are generally imprecise, leaving the reader to decide exactly what the writer means.

Mixed metaphor   Two metaphors which contradict each other or for some other reason are not appropriate when used together. Such thoughtless expressions invite ridicule.

Modify   To describe further the meaning of another word. (In the sentence just finished *further* modifies *describe*.) Adjectives modify nouns or pronouns; adverbs modify verbs, adjectives or other adverbs. The modifier, and that which

---

	it modifies, may be a clause or phrase rather than an individual word.
Mood	The form of a verb that tells whether the action it describes is fact (indicative mood), command (imperative mood) or condition contrary to fact (subjunctive mood).
Nominative	The form (case) of a pronoun which denotes that it is the subject of its sentence.
Object	The noun or pronoun which receives the action of a verb, or which is governed by a preposition.
Objective	The form (case) of a pronoun which denotes that it is an object in its sentence.
Participle	A word derived from a verb but used as an adjective, because it participates as both. Commonly used as a simple adjective. Also, the latter part of a verb, following some form of 'to be'.
Passive voice	The intransitive verb form in which the subject receives the action of the verb. The object (of a preposition) performs the action, or there may be no object and hence no stated source of the action.

Perfect	The verb form which denotes that the action reported by that verb was completed at the time being reported.
Phrase	A group of words lacking a subject or a verb, or both. (Distinguished from a *clause*, which must have a subject and a verb.)
Possessive	The form (case) of a noun or pronoun which denotes possession. Singular nouns are made possessive simply by adding -'s.
Predicate	The main verb of a sentence or clause, which makes some statement about its subject.
Restrictive clause	A dependent (subordinate) clause which limits the meaning of the main clause.
Sentence	A group of words containing at least one independent clause, and beginning with a capital letter and ending with a full stop (or other ending punctuation). Its subject or verb may be implied, instead of being explicitly stated.
Sentence fragment	A part of a sentence standing as a sentence (as here). There are two rules:

1. Keep them short, so the reader can tell that the omission is deliberate.

2. Only use them occasionally – the reader will feel uncomfortable if conventional patterns are broken too often.

Simile
A group of words that makes a direct comparison to something else, usually to create a more accurate image.

Simple sentence
A sentence containing one independent clause and no dependent clauses. A simple sentence may be complicated. It may contain phrases, compound subject or verb, and several modifiers.

Slang
Informal language, unsuitable in business writing.

Subject
The part of a sentence or clause which most closely connects with the main verb (predicate), either by performing or receiving the action of that verb. The subject is usually a noun or pronoun, but may also be a gerund.

Subjunctive
The form (mood) of a verb which denotes that the action or condition described by that verb is contrary to fact.

Syntax
Sentence structure.

Tense
The form of a verb which denotes whether the

action it describes is in the past, present or future.

Transitive verb   One that needs an object (direct object) to complete its meaning. The most commonly used sentence structure is: subject, transitive verb, direct object.

Verbal   A word formed from a verb but used as something else. The three common types of verbals are gerunds, infinitives and participles.

Voice   The form of a verb which tells whether the subject performs the action that the verb describes (active voice), or receives it (passive voice).